9—12

From:

George W.

Simmons Jr.

A Determined Man

An Autobiography by
George W. Simmons, Jr.

First Printing-March 1997
500 Copies
Second Printing- October 1997
500 Copies
Printed in U.S.A.

Kentucky Color Publishing
P.O. Box 4026
Frankfort, Kentucky 40604

I.S.B.N. 0-9651653-1-0

A Determined Man

by

George W. Simmons, Jr.

DEDICATION

Mother, O Mother of love divine.
You carried us in your heart.
The prayers you offered to God for us
Will never from us depart.

(Author Unknown)

This Book is Respectfully Dedicated to my Mother.

The Builder

An old man going a long highway
Came at an evening cold and gray,
Came to a chasm vast, deep, and wide.
The old man crossed in the twilight dim.
The sullen stream had no fear for him.
He paused when safe on the other side,
And built a bridge to stem the tide.

"Old man," said a fellow pilgrim near,
"You're wasting your time building here.
Your journey ends with the close of day.
You never again shall pass this way.
You've crossed the chasm vast, and deep, and wide.
Why build you this bridge at eventide?"

The builder lifted his old gray head.
"Good friend, in the past I have come," he said.
"There followeth after me today
A youth whose feet must pass this way.
He too, must cross in the twilight dim.
Good friend, I'm building this bridge for him."

(Author Unknown)

BOYHOOD DAYS

Chapter 1

It's not a matter of where you were born
Or when you were born;
But it's what's born when you're born.

(Author Unknown)

꙰꙰꙰꙰꙰꙰꙰꙰꙰꙰꙰

Chapter 1

BOYHOOD DAYS

I was born in Tehula, Holmes County, Mississippi, on October 15, 1911. My parents moved from this community when I was two years old. We moved to Darling, in Quitman County, Mississippi. In fact, we were three miles east of Darling on Squirrel Lake. The name Squirrel Lake came from the first inhabitants who said they never saw so many squirrels per acre before. Darling had a population of approximately three hundred. Our Post Office Box was #46. To receive a special delivery or telegram was unknown. We went to town about once a week, mostly on Saturday afternoon; it depended largely on whether the farm crops were cultivated up to par.

We are not sure of what path, or paths, led Alec and Adline Cade and Addison and Dinah Simmons to Meridian, Mississippi and Tehula, Mississippi. We do know that Alec Cade was a direct descendant of an Indian tribe. The Cades were parents of eight children, including: Willie, Lillie, Pricilla, Lemmie, Corrie, Toug and Annie. The Simmons were also parents of a brood of eight, including: Eugene, Ella, George, Callie, Pearl, Hagty and Lovy. In their blossoming years, my father, George Simmons, Sr., was attracted to Corrie Cade by sight. He had never actually met her, but told his mother that he would some day marry this young woman that he saw frequently from afar. However, Corrie Cade had other plans. She married Mose Smith. Mose was a fireman on the railroad. His job kept him on the road and "playing the field." After a few years of uncertainty and loneliness, Corrie was left alone with their young son, Willie Mercy.

When Mrs. "Corrie" Cade Smith was again ready to receive company, she was convinced that George W. Simmons was the one with whom she wanted to spend the rest of her life. George W. Simmons and Corrie Cade Smith were married in 1909. George was just the father that Willie Mercy needed. After living with the Addison Simmons' family a while, the newly wedded couple wanted to start their own family. The first child was still-born. In Tehula they welcomed their second son and named him George W. Simmons, Jr., as they had planned for the first born. "Mr. Simmons" and "Miss Corrie," as they called each other, were now ready to venture out and make their own little nest. They bought forty acres of land with two houses: one with two rooms and kitchen and the other with three rooms and kitchen. As the family increased, Dad found it necessary to add two more rooms to the house in which we lived. All of the remaining members of the George and Corrie Simmons clan were born while living on this forty acre farm. They were: Etha Mae, Niculia, Maceo Addison, Mamie Ophell, Corrie Lee, and . Lillian Elizabeth. All were delivered by Corrie's sister Lillie who was the area midwife. George's sister, Lovy, died in childbirth one month after Etha Mae was born; therefore, Corrie was the natural person to take "Bessie Mae," as the orphan was named, to appear as Etha's twin. Willie Mercy lived in Jackson, Tennessee with Dad's sister Callie throughout his high school career.

Our parents were very much impressed with the city school system, compared to that of the Squirrel Lake, Mississippi system. They were so impressed that they made arrangements for me to attend school in Jackson during Willie Mercy's senior year. I didn't want to stay in Jackson the first year, but they bought me an overcoat in order to satisfy me. It was oxford grey and cost three dollars and a half ($3.50). This was the first overcoat I ever owned. But when Willie M., as we called him, decided to go to Alcorn College in Alcorn, Mississippi, I was no longer interested in staying in Jackson. As I was so dissatisfied, they came to Jackson and took me back to Squirrel Lake in time for me to enroll in school in September.

Very few farmers realized how important it was to paint houses back in those days. A few mixed lime with water and applied it to other buildings on the farm; some even white-washed their picket fences. This method made a nice appearance as long as the sun shined, but when the rain came it didn't look the same; instead of being white, it appeared dirty-like white. Building houses back in those days was quite different than today. Solid foundations such as concrete, concrete block, or bricks were unknown. Wood blocks cut from trees similar to those we now use for wood heating purposes were used for foundations. The length of the block determined how high one wanted his structure from the ground. The space underneath the house we used for storage for certain tools. The space also served as shelter for hogs during the winter. Tin roofs were quite popular back in those days. It might sound unbelievable, but when it rained on the tin roof we slept much better until the roof started leaking. I have pushed the bed over, out of the rain, many a night and placed a container under the leak.

When all farm crops in the community were gathered, or harvested, all livestock was turned out into the fields where they found much food such as corn and other grain that was overlooked during harvest. A mule or horse was always kept in the lot to be ridden to search for those that were out during the day. Most had no fences; therefore, when livestock was turned out during the day, they were free to go wherever they chose. Bells were placed on mules' and cows' necks in order to identify them in mid-afternoon. Most farmers knew their bell tone, but they were sometimes misled as others sounded similar to someone else's bell, which had almost the same tone. It might be interesting to know that each farmer's livestock were usually found together, both mules and cows. Occasionally they were joined by others. But wherever they were found, they were easily separated from others; in fact, if and when they saw the owner coming, they were like children who were picked up at the playground or day-care center by their parents.

Seldom did hogs run with mules or cows. In fact, in most cases, they did not go as far as the larger animals. Sometimes they were within calling distance and were given extra food on arrival as a token of appreciation for having come home on their own. After the evening's feed, many hogs chose to sleep under the house instead of going to the hog pen where they were restricted during early spring when crops were planted. As the houses were built approximately two feet above ground level, it not only served as shelter for hogs, but many farming tools were also kept under the house. It was not uncommon for pigs to fight for positions with their mothers during cold weather at night as well as at nursing time; big pigs pushed the smaller ones away from the sow's udder. We, as children, too had problems at bedtime competing for positions as it became necessary for three or four to share the same bed, especially when we had company. Our biggest complaint was when one at the opposite end of the bed put his feet in one's face. This all happened before the addition was added to the house.

We always looked forward to the day when company came so that we might sleep on a pallet and eat foods during the weekdays that we seldom got otherwise until Sunday. The guests were sometimes too many for everyone to eat at the same time. Therefore, the children had to be last to eat. When meats were served, we could always bet on enough rice and gravy, even though the meat was limited. In case steak was served, mother would always divide it in order that each of us got his fair share. In case of chicken being served, we could always get such parts as heads, including the neck, as well as the feet and wings. Coffee was kept in the house, but it was served only to those visitors who preferred it. We were permitted to drink hot water with just enough coffee to color the water.

Canned foods were very popular during those days, and mother canned everything imaginable. We grew turnips and sweet potatoes as well as other vegetables by the bushels. We ate turnips from the time of maturity until almost time for the following year's crop. In fact, I should never want to see another turnip (bottom). When turnips reached a stage of maturity, we harvested them and heaped them on straw around a pole approximately five feet tall and four or five inches in diameter in a geometrical cone-like shape. Afterwards, they were covered with straw about six or eight inches in diameter, and seasoned or dried corn stalks were placed over the straw. The corn stalks were covered with dirt about eight or ten inches for protection from winter weather. A hole approximately twelve inches in diameter was left on the southside for one who wanted to get a mess of turnips when the need arose. This hole was covered with some sort of material such as an old rug, and solid material was placed over this in order to protect the turnips from falling weather. The south side was preferable as the north wind was usually the colder during winter. The above mentioned system was used to protect sweet potatoes also.

Vacation and retirement were for white people only. We always looked forward to laying the crop by July Fourth. That is, weeds and grass had been kept away from the farm crops, such as cotton (the main crop), corn, sorghum, and vegetables, which by this time had grown so tall the grass and weeds were unable to survive because of the lack of food, water, and sunlight. Sometimes this schedule was not accomplished because of rainy weather which delayed working on the farm.

4

But the Fourth of July was always celebrated in the form of a picnic, baseball game, or both. In most cases, fish and squirrel were the meats, and lemonade was the drink. A select group went to the lake, caught the fish, and dressed it; another group killed squirrels; and a third group prepared a barrel of lemonade. The meat was cooked in a wash pot used to boil clothes, and lemonade was made in a fifty or fifty-five gallon barrel. All of this had to done on the same day of the picnic because refrigeration was unknown. Ice was purchased in blocks (25, 50, or 100 pounds) and had to be preserved by covering it with sawdust and some form of cloth. All of this took place on the lake near the ball diamond so that those who were interested in the game could eat while watching the game.

Usually, the game was played between the local team and one invited from another community. We had no uniform or equipment. We played in our regular clothing (usually overalls), and caught the ball barehanded or with a small garment, especially the catcher behind the batter. We made our own balls, usually of cord string. Sometimes a small rubber ball was inside the cord, and the finished ball was sewn with a big needle and coarse thread. Occasionally the game had to be called off if the ball was beat to a frazzle and we didn't have another. We made our own bats from a twig or branchlet from a tree (oak, ash or hickory). After having trimmed it with a knife to the desired shape, glass was used to smooth the handle to the desired size. Sometimes we were lucky enough to obtain a catcher's mitt; otherwise, the catcher had to use a garment, such as a coat or sweater. Being a center fielder, I caught with bare hands. We had no gloves, mitts or bats and sometime no ball, and played in our everyday clothing. We caught the ball in our garments such as jackets, sweaters, and coats, and some parents did not allow their children to use their belongings for such. Therefore, they were forced to catch the ball with bare hands; many times when the pitcher threw a wild pitch, the catcher threw the garment where the ball was thrown whether in the air or on the ground to find that it landed in the pocket or sleeve of the garment which he caught with. The game was sometimes delayed until the ball was patched. Needles and thread were always available for the occasion. The balls were made of twine which was wrapped around a small size rubber ball or a stone, which caused the ball to be quite flabby as a result of blows from the bat. Occasionally the game was called off because the ball had worn out or been lost. Therefore, whoever was in lead at such a time was considered the winner.

Our baseball season was determined by weather conditions, that is, we played until late fall, but the big day always came on the fourth of July. Football, softball and basketball were unknown. I thought I was an outstanding baseball player and frequently participated in the game until they started playing on Sunday. At that time I had to stop because I was not allowed to play ball on Sunday; therefore, I had to give up baseball. Occasionally I played on Sunday, with fear that my parents would find it out, and I knew what came next. If I did slip out and play when my parents were not around, it did not occur often. And in case neighbors or friends of the family caught one going against the rules, they reported it, and one was in trouble. I was told many times that I should be in the big league. Like all other walks of life, there were many blacks qualified for the professional games, but were refused because of the color of their skin. The poet has so beautifully said, *"The laws of changeless justice binds, oppressors with oppressed and close as sin and suffering join we march to fate abreast."* Even though my numerous setbacks were hard to bear, I kept the faith and came through with flying colors, thanks be to God.

Many times I got up early in the morning, saddled old Mike, our riding mule, and rode three miles to Darling, Mississippi to purchase six shotgun shells for twenty five cents in order to go hunting. I was not able to afford a box of shells though they cost less than a dollar. This meant I couldn't afford to fire at will; instead of firing at a rabbit that jumped up before me, I called the dogs, put them on the track, and waited quietly until they trailed him back within shooting distance. At that time he would be so far in front of the dogs he would not be running very fast. In fact, he usually would run a short distance and wait to listen in order to find out how far the dogs were behind. And mind you, back in those days the hunt was not just for sport, but food to go on the family table. Therefore, it behooved me to make every shot count. We've eaten rabbits and you name it. Such animals were prepared various ways, with dumplings, rice and gravy, etc.

A few fellows in the community at least had a hunting jacket in order to carry whatever game killed, but I couldn't afford this luxury. Therefore, I had to put a belt around my waist, and whatever my game, it was attached to the belt by

6

head or feet, whichever one was spared when it was killed. During that time we did not know anything about a hunting suit; we hunted in whatever we had. When one returned home after the hunt, his trousers were filled with blood. Today, I have a hunting outfit, from head to feet. My hunting outfit is equipped to carry a box of shells, twenty-five to be exact, and a jacket equipped to carry the game.

Occasionally the dogs chased a rabbit so closely, he ran to a tree which was decayed from the ground up to approximately two or three feet from the inside and the rabbit rushed to this point and went into the decayed area for refuge. When the dog reached this point, he went no further, but remained there and barked constantly until the huntsman reached this point. There were two ways by which the rabbit could be apprehended: either by smoke or a branch from a tree, long enough to reach the rabbit. In case one had matches, the smoke method was used. That is, a fire was made at the base of the tree, just enough to produce the amount of smoke to force the rabbit to fall to the ground. In case we had no matches, we cut a branch long enough to reach the rabbit and twisted it into his fur and we pulled him to the ground.

I did quite a bit of coon hunting too. We had dogs for rabbits, raccoons and squirrels. Rabbits and squirrels were hunted during the day, and in case a dog was used for squirrels, they were hunted similar to rabbits. They seldom went into holes in the trees, but in their own nests, which were built for refuge as well as shelter out of the weather. In case one preferred to hunt squirrels without dogs, the best time to hunt them was early in the morning about the break of day or late in the afternoon, just before dark or in case of rain most anytime during the day right after the rain. Raccoons were hunted only at night, with dogs; otherwise, they were not to be found. When found by the dogs, they were only trailed until they got tired of running and took a tree for refuge. And in order to capture the raccoon, one had to see the glare from his eyes as he looked down from the tree. Occasionally, one seemed aware that he exposed himself by looking down and refused to look, which caused the huntsman to remain at the scene until the break of day in order to capture the raccoon. Many times the raccoon would come down to the ground at daybreak at which time the huntsman would fail to shoot it, but allow the dogs to kill it. Sometime if there was only one dog to challenge the raccoon, he might lose the fight in favor of the raccoon. Therefore, it forced the huntsman to shoot him. We also ran across opossum. They were just the opposite when it came to defending themselves against their enemies. Instead of offering resistance, they gave up immediately by playing dead. I've sold many a hide, or skin, from both raccoons and opossum. The latter brought less, but every penny counted with me during those days. Hides from rattlesnakes brought a pretty good price too; their skins were used mostly for making belts.

I've seen the time when I owned as many as eleven dogs, one for every occasion. This might seem expensive, but we lived on the farm where we grew most everything except sugar, flour, salt and baking powder. Therefore, we fed dogs almost like we fed other livestock. One could always tell when such animals died, like cows, mules, etc., because they were taken to the woods where buzzards, dogs and opossum consumed the carcasses. We always regretted when the wind blew from the direction where such animals were left to come in the direction of our dwellings.. I sometimes wonder just how we did make it this far in the midst of flies, mosquitoes, bedbugs, and outhouses where one went to eliminate. One went into the doorway, which had no door, as *per se*, but a cloth hung from the top of the doorway to keep one from being seen from the outside and when one went into the front door. The chickens joined the individual, only they went to the back in order to feed from whatever feces that became available during the process. Doctors were almost as scarce as "hen's teeth." In fact, our parents took care of our physical needs with home remedies. I don't eat opossums anymore, in fact, I don't enjoy wild meat like I use to. Wives can make husbands like or dislike anything they want to. Kentucky Fried Chicken is famous throughout the world, and chickens will eat anything an opossum will eat. Colette (1873-1954), a French novelist said, "Look for a long time at what pleases you, and for a longer time at what pains you."

During the months of July and August, we always looked forward to harvesting the sorghum for molasses and cutting winter wood. When the sorghum was harvested, we loaded it on the wagon and took it to the sorghum mill which was centrally located in the community. The man who made the molasses gave each person or family a location at which to unload, and your molasses was made in the order in which you came. In order to protect the sorghum from moisture, while you waited your turn (especially during rainy weather), wood was placed on

8

the ground on which the sorghum (cane) was stacked. Stakes were placed in the ground (usually four) in order to hold the sorghum in place until your turn came to process or grind the juice from the stalk and cook it into molasses. Mules or horses were used to pull the mill, and each family furnished its own team. The sorghum was fed into the mill by a member or members of the family involved. As youngsters, we were exposed to the latest gossip and old jokes, but sometimes we pretended that we were not listening. I always looked forward to going to the molasses mill when the time came. Once the sorghum was taken to the mill, the process was easier from then on.

We made around forty or fifty gallons a year. This might sound like a lot of molasses; however, when a family of nine or ten members ate molasses two or maybe three times a day for eight or ten months a year, we didn't have any to turn to sugar. Many meals consisted of bread and molasses, with butter whipped into the molasses. Occasionally, I poured bacon grease into the molasses for a change. We often had cornbread and milk. I liked sugar in buttermilk and cornbread, but we couldn't afford sugar as often as we liked. I sometimes put sorghum molasses in my milk and bread. Even though it looked like slop for hogs, I enjoyed it for a change.

Cutting winter wood for the home during the months of July and August served two purposes: in the first place, the roads were good during this time of year as they consisted of dirt (not even gravel), and one didn't have to worry about getting stuck between the place where the wood was cut and the house. Sometimes the wood ran out before the winter was over, and one could not put a full load on the wagon. We tried it many times to find we got stuck in the mud and had to throw half of the load off and go home with a half load and return to pick up the other half later. Secondly, work on the farm was very light during this time of waiting for the cotton picking season in late August or early September. Occasionally we had hay ready during this time for harvest. I even tried cutting cord wood during this season, but it was a bit too much for me with that four-cutter Simon saw. My half brother often complained about me riding the saw. When I became tired, he said I rode the saw; that is, I leaned too much on the saw, and as he pulled it he had to pull me too.

We also picked blackberries during this season. Mother canned many a gallon. There were very few orchards in our area (the Delta), but some five or six miles away, in the hills, all kinds of fruits were grown. Occasionally, we went to the hills and picked fruit, as it was much cheaper when you picked your own. Going to the hills was an exciting time of the year for us. We always got an early start (by daybreak). We hitched the mules to the wagon and put tubs, lard cans, and buckets in the wagon. All these were filled, and mother would can fruit for the next day or two. Our mules, like us, were not accustomed to going up and down the hills; therefore, we had to take a chain or rope to tie the back wheels to the wagon bed to prevent turning while going down hills.

Around the latter part of August and the first of September, cotton began to open (that is, the lent or soft fibrous material began to open), and each farmer decided according to what percent opened as to when to start picking. The criteria was to not start unless a bale could be picked over a given area. A bale weighed from eleven hundred to fifteen hundred pounds, depending on the brand grown. Most farmers had cotton houses, that is, storage space. The cotton was weighed as picked, and when a bale was picked it was loaded on the wagon. The side boards used were approximately five feet tall in order to take the cotton to the gin. There the seeds were separated from the lent, and the cotton and seed were readied for the market. If the farmer was satisfied with the crop, he kept enough seed for the following year's crop; but if not, he sold them. Like other produce, the market fluctuated, and the farmers watched the prices and sold when they felt the price was right.

Sometimes the cotton opened faster than we could pick it; therefore, it became necessary to start pulling the whole bale about an hour or two before dark. We took it to the house and picked it after the regular chores were done and dinner was over. I've hitched the mules to the wagon many times around two or three o'clock and then driven three miles to the gin in Darling, to find several wagons already in line at the gin stand waiting their turn. Many times I've returned home around midnight, fed the mules, eaten, gone to bed; and it seemed as though by the time I closed my eyes it was time to get up and start all over again. Mother was my best supporter. She said many times, *"Son, keep on keeping on, there's a better day ahead."* I didn't tell her, but as I grew older the days "seemed darker and drearier."

September didn't mean a thing so far as school was concerned unless the crops were harvested. And bad weather kept us out of school sometimes. Early in March it was time to prepare the soil for the next crop and to plant such crops as corn and hay. The first of April was cotton planting time. We, as boys, were lucky if we got five or six months in school each year. Therefore, I was forced the following year to go back and start all over again. Dad, being a minister, spent much time away from home in his ministerial work, such as revivals or conventions. I've put saddles on two mules many days to take home to Darling to catch the train to fulfill his mission and by the same token, picked him up on return maybe a week or ten days later. Even though I had to harness the mule and return to the field, this gave me a break in between. I led one mule and rode the other during the transportation process. Many times when we returned home, I unsaddled the mules and harnessed them for plowing. Dad would plow an hour or two then hitch his mule to the fence, go to the house and go to bed. When noon hour came, I took both mules to the house, fed them, and took a little nap (around thirty minutes) before dinner was ready.

Most parents who lived in the community on Squirrel Lake were always glad when summer or spring came in late March or the first of April, so that we could go barefooted. This was good economy, but we always dreaded having to wash our feet at bedtime. Saturday night was bathtime. Whoever said, "I'm first," was first to bathe, and others came in the order in which they voted. In looking back, it's unbelievable that we survived. We had to pump extra water for baths, and it had to be heated on the stove. We bathed in the wash tub which had to be placed as close as possible to the stove or fireplace during winter months. Sometimes one was reminded that the butt was too close to the fire when he touched that side of the tub next to the heat. Regardless of the type job done on the farm or how sweaty one became while doing the job, one never got that bath but once a week (Saturday night).

I would sleep on the floor, but it was necessary to put some form of protection over my face as a protective means from the flies. This was also true at mealtime; someone had to constantly fan flies while we ate. We had no screens,

11

and windows had to be raised for air. Chickens also came in through windows in search of food that was sometimes left on the table. Mice and rats were also prevalent, and most farmers had house cats that took care of the mice. But they couldn't handle the rats that were found around the barnyard and where corn and other grain were stored. In this case, we set traps and caught many.

I did much fishing and hunting too. Our fishing equipment consisted of a pole (cane), which grew in the community. Everyone selected his own, and a large bottle cork was used as a float. The only thing to be purchased at the store was twine, lead, and hooks; a grass-sack or gunny sack (of which most farmers had many) was used to carry the catch. We also did quite a bit of frog hunting. The only necessary tools or equipment for frog hunting were a light (lantern or headlight because flashlights were a rarity) and a gig (this was a tool with prongs similar to a pitch fork, but not as large) with a long handle. Frogs (similar to raccoons and opossums) are hunted at night, and the light blinds them which enables the hunter to quietly come within gigging range in order to gig him. We hunted raccoons and opossums at night and rabbits during the day. It was much fun if one had good dogs.

When the dogs found raccoons or opossums, they chased them until they climbed a tree. The hunter was always made aware when these animals went up the tree; the dogs would never leave the tree, and they changed the tune of their voices as they barked. A good dog would never leave the tree until the game was killed or the hunter led the dog away from the tree on a leash. A raccoon is very smart. Unless the dog was very close on its trail, it climbed down from the tree and kept going. This confused some dogs, especially young dogs with little experience who stopped at the first tree thinking the raccoon was still there. But the well-trained dog circled the tree repeatedly to make sure the raccoon was still there. We tried to always make sure the dog had found that the coon was there by waiting until the dog refused to leave the tree. At that time we followed through to the tree in search of the raccoon. Before carbide lights were invented, we had to use the old-fashioned kerosene head light. The raccoon had to look down so that one could see the glare in his eyes, but an old raccoon was aware of this and therefore would not look down. We sometimes made a fire under the tree which excited the raccoon, and he came down in spite of the dogs and huntsman. In case of only one dog, he might whip the dog and escape if not shot. Opossums were not too smart; if caught before they got to a tree, they played (possum) dead.

Time spent in the woods on a given night depended on many things, such as the amount of game found within a given time. If hunting was good, we'd maybe spend the night in the woods, especially if we had nothing to do on the farm the following day. If the weather was extremely cold, we made a fire, and in case of rain (if not too hard), it was OK because we always thought the dogs could trail the game much better. But at the end of the hunt, we called the dogs in with a horn made from cows horn, went home, and left the game to be cleaned the next morning. We sold the fur and ate the rest. Fur from a raccoon was worth seventy-five or eighty cents, while that from a possum sold for around fifty or sixty cents. There was a standard by which each of these hides had to be stretched in order to be sold.

The only difference between rabbit hunting and the above is that rabbits are hunted during the daylight. The same dog that hunted at night would seldom hunt rabbits. When the dogs are trailing a rabbit, it is a proven fact that he usually completes a cycle, if it's not killed before. The rabbit hunter who follows this pattern usually has the better chance at catching the rabbit. Rabbits sometimes go into a hollow tree if chased too closely. The rabbit dog would trail him to this point and usually remain there until the huntsman arrived. I've made many a smoke at the base of the tree and covered it with a garment until the rabbit reached the point he could no longer stand the smoke and coughed a few times before falling.

Mother was an expert when it came to economizing in every respect. We had rabbit with rice and gravy as well as dumplings. The liver from rabbits seldom reached the kitchen; as soon as the rabbit was dressed, we put it on coals of fire in front of the fireplace, and we thought it was better than if it had been cooked in the kitchen. We always looked forward for Mother to prepare a raccoon with sweet potatoes, but opossums were not so tasty when we found out their eating habits. However, we still like fried chicken and country ham, and these had the same eating habits as that of a possum.

Early fall, in November or sometimes as late as December, was hog killing time. In order to prepare the hog for home consumption, it was placed in a fattening pen with limited space and wood floor and was fed nothing but corn. This prevented rooting in the ground getting too much exercise to throw off weight. It took around six or eight weeks to prepare for killing time.

Killing time varied with different farmers. We helped each other; whichever one killed first could always depend on the neighbor's help. No money was ever involved, meat only. When the killing was over, the hog was hung on a scaffold overnight to chill, and the farmer used his own method in the curing process. Some smoked while others salted for a given period, then the meat was hung in the smokehouse, convenient to the kitchen where the cook always took the butcher's knife and cut whatever she wanted the time being. This same method was used in killing beef.

We always looked forward to claiming the bladder from hogs in order to blow them up as balloons. When painted they looked just like any other balloon, only the surface was rough. This was a part of our Christmas decoration. I can recall many times when I had a taste for a bite or two from the hams after they were cured. I took a knife to the smoke house and sliced from the lean part, real smoothly so it appeared to have been sliced by the cook.

Everyone had chores around the house; mine was to be the first one to get up in the morning, make fires in the girls' room and our parents' room and the kitchen so that the stove would be heating while others got dressed. From there I fed the livestock and milked the cows. If breakfast was not ready by the time the sun rose, we went to the field first, especially during the rush season when unfavorable weather prevented farmers from getting the farm work done on schedule. For example, during an unusually rainy season, whether it be during cultivation or harvest, it was impossible to cope with grass and weeds. I recall many times having harnessed the mule, gone to the field and plowed approximately an hour before breakfast was ready. When breakfast was ready, mother placed a white cloth on a fishing pole and placed it where it could be seen, especially when one was not within calling distance. While preparing breakfast, Mother sometimes found it convenient to put a few sweet potatoes and peanuts in the oven to go along with the noon meal. As soon as breakfast was over, you mounted your mule, or horse, whatever, went back to the field and plowed until noon. At 1:00 p.m. it was time to go back to the field until just before dark, allowing enough time to do chores around the house such as milking cows, feeding the livestock, and taking the wood into the house.

We knew nothing about a "child labor law." The job was assigned by our parents, according to the size and ability. When the cornmeal was almost depleted, we shelled the corn and took it to the grist mill to be ground into meal. When I started to going to the mill, I was so small Dad had to place the sack which contained the corn on the mule, equally distributed on either side of the saddle, and when I arrived at the mill, someone would take it off the mule. If work was not up to par on the farm, we were instructed not to wait if there were too many ahead at the mill, but request for a swap (or trade corn) for meal already ground and return to the farm immediately.

Willie M. and I were never able to understand why we left the forty-acre farm on Squirrel Lake in Mississippi, because it was there where we enjoyed independence and accomplished more in the way of livelihood. Money was scarce, but we had more in the way of freedom and independence. We left Squirrel Lake in 1927.

From there we moved to Cold Water River. This is where freedom and independence vanished. This is where the "Do's and Don'ts" are issued by the plantation owner. Not only are you told what to grow, but how much to grow. For example, farmers in Mississippi placed special interest in cotton. Very few plantation owners permitted tenant farmers to own cattle and hogs; perhaps a few chickens were permitted. "King Cotton," corn, and hay were the major crops. Mother worked on the farm right along with the rest of the family. She prepared breakfast, and when we finished eating we took off back to the field. We sometimes went to the field before breakfast was ready and were notified when it was ready. Around ten thirty or eleven o'clock, Mother went to the house to prepare the mid-day meal.

We did everything together as a family. Before eating, we went to the wash pan which was located conveniently to the kitchen, poured water from the water bucket, and washed hands and face with our hands. We knew nothing about a face towel except the one which hung on the wall, and it was used to dry face and hands on. Many times when one went to dry, he searched to see which was the most appropriate place on the towel to dry. We used a dipper or gourd to dip

15

the water from the bucket to wash or drink with. The policy at our house was that if the one who went to take water from the bucket found it was just about depleted, he was to go to the pump and replenish it. Therefore, everyone was cautious in order not to be the one to go to the pump. The pump sometimes had to be primed; therefore, in this case, a small container was kept nearby with water in it in order to prime the pump. Many times whoever went to draw water took what was left in the bucket to prime the pump in case the container at the pump was empty. In order to get cool water, the pump had to be pumped a minute or two before pumping water for the house consumption. Water for the livestock was also supplied from this pump. Our parents often checked the containers from which the livestock drank because no one wanted to take time to do the pumping since it took much water to supply the need for the mules, cows, hogs, and chickens. Some members of the family thought the move from Squirrel Lake was wise for educational reasons; the schools were not the very best. However, I always thought that *it mattered not where one was born, but what's born when you were born.*

We fought muskeaters during the summer and bedbugs sometimes throughout the year. We had to make smokes during summer for both family and livestock (except hogs) in the evenings. As soon as the smoke was made, the animals came running. And the family smoke was made at a central location convenient for all to share. Many times we had limited screens and had to leave doors or windows open in order to get air. One thing in our favor was that we only had one-on-one between flies and mosquitoes; we fought flies during the day and mosquitoes at night. But in case one didn't have a mosquito net over his bed to protect him, he had both bed bugs and mosquitoes. It was common for one to wake up during the night, strike a match, and see bedbugs running in all directions and blood on bedding. We always looked forward to taking the bedding as well as the beds out and trying to rid them of bedbugs in springtime.

I've seen many a time when I went to the ten cent store and purchased half soles for my shoes for thirty-five cents and did my own half sole with glue and a ruffner, similar to the way we used to patch an innertube for an automobile. I've also taken a string or wire and tied it across the toe of my shoes where the sole had started pulling away from the shoe. When my shoes were black and we couldn't afford shoe polish, which cost ten or fifteen cents, I took soot from the stove pipe, mixed water with it, and applied it to my shoes; the shoes wouldn't shine, but they were at least black. We purchased socks for ten or fifteen cents, and when the heels wore out I'd tuck the toe underneath so the heel would not show.

Many times during mid summer I had to wear a coat (while others were in their shirt sleeves) in order to hide a hole in my shirt or the patch Mother had placed over the hole in the back or on the shoulders. I was grown when I went to the barber shop for a haircut. It was always someone in the community who cut hair, and the cost for a haircut was ten or fifteen cents. Boys during those times wore long hair, similar to today; Mother, having been a beautician, straightened mine similar to the way she did for the ladies. Many Saturday nights I fought sleep waiting for her to finish with her last customer in order for her to get mine before midnight. After midnight on Saturday, all work ceased at our house except those essential jobs such as taking care of the livestock (feeding and milking). Weekend wood for the house had to be cut on Saturday, if not before. Most of our garments were made by Mother with her sewing machine. She made dresses for the girls and shirts for the men folks, curtains, bedspreads, and mattresses (the old fashioned type with the split down the center from near the head to the foot). This split made it convenient to equalize or spread as evenly as possible, the straw, cotton, or corn shucks which the mattress contained. For a number of years I suffered from athletes foot (Trichophytosis) as a result of shoes, secondhand, which someone gave me as a favor. This was my first knowledge of name brand shoes, such as Florsheims, or Stacy Adams.

Health facilities, for blacks, were few and far between. I recall an instance when I suffered quite a bit from a toothache; many times whether at work or play I had to go home so that mother would saturate cotton with Slone's Liniment and place it into the cavity for temporary relief. This occurred so frequently, and I had so many cavities that it was obvious that something had to be done. The nearest Black dentist was located in Clarksdale, Mississippi, thirteen miles away. Mother suggested that I take two hens to Clarksdale, and hopefully the dentist would pull all necessary teeth and treat those that could be saved. The next day she gave me two Plymouth hens, and I placed each under my arms and hitchhiked to Clarksdale to a dentist who did the job for the chickens. This made me very happy. We could

17

not even afford a toothbrush or toothpaste; many times we used twigs from a small branch of the tree for the brush and baking soda, which was sometimes mixed with salt, to clean our teeth. We also used baking soda as a deodorant after we took baths.

Many times I looked forward to rushing home after school closed in order that Mother could wash my trousers (that should have been dry cleaned) so that I could press them before midnight Saturday in order to wear them to church on Sunday. They were sometimes patched in the seat. Button shoes were popular during those days; one with button shoes had to have a shoebuttoner in order to button the shoes, and sometimes a button came off and had to be replaced with an odd button if the others could not be matched. In case of shoes with laces, if the lace was broken within the midsection, it could be tied and hide the knot in the center. Boots were a necessity on the farm; everyone had to have them during winter months in order to get outside the house. Most people wore knee boots; only a few wore hip boots. I always appreciated whatever I had, large or small. When Dad bought a pair of boots for me, I was as happy as could be. At bedtime I'd place them beside my bed, close enough to be reached during the night, so that I could feel them in the dark. My wife teases me at times when I purchase a new pair of shoes, bring them home, place them in the middle of the bed, and take a step or two backward and look them over from all angles.

The early stage of my social life with the girls was somewhat complicated. I was not allowed to call on the girls until I was around eighteen years of age. While others, both boys and girls were dating around sixteen or seventeen. Having to slip around with the girls was quite a handicap; they wanted to be seen with their favorite boyfriends out in the eyes of the public, and I wanted to be one among that number. But it was almost impossible, because everyone in the community could and would identify you to your parents in case you were caught. Taboo, in this case, was a hard word to accept, "to take when offered; agree to; receive with favor or willingness." We were not taught sex by our parents. (I remember once when Dad caught dogs breeding at our house, he took his shot gun and killed each of them.) The only thing I was familiar with was the shot gun wedding; that is in case you got some girl pregnant you'd better marry her and consider yourself lucky to get by with that in the sight of her parents.

My first, intelligent, knowledge of sex came by the way of my grade school teacher who looked at me and felt that I was in dire need of information pertaining to sex. I was always the oldest member of my classes and she gave me a book on sex and suggested that I read it without discussing it with others for fear someone would be misled regarding her motive. This meant more to me at that time than any lesson in science, because I was getting the wrong information pertaining to sex at that time. For example, I was being taught masturbation and felt that this was one way to satisfy sexual desire without fear of getting a baby or venereal disease (VD). But I didn't realize that this was a form of sexual self-abuse. When I finished the book, I returned it to the teacher and thanked her without further discussion, because we both knew this was a taboo not only with my parents, but many others in that community. I hardly knew just which direction to turn from this point. But I consider myself very fortunate to not come up with V.D.

When we went out on dates, Sunday was dating time; when we left home Sunday morning for Sunday School and regular morning service, we called it morning service. But it seldom started before twelve o'clock and lasted until late. We were not allowed to sit with our dates in church, but when it came time to raise the offering, we walked up to the collection table, put a nickel in church and went where our girlfriends sat and gave them a nickel to put in the collection. Very seldom I had more than a quarter on Sunday, and it was broken down to four nickels and five pennies: a penny for Sunday School, two nickels for church, for you and your date. We very seldom visited our dates immediately after the church service. In between that time for the afternoon dates we went by the country store and purchased a coke for five cents and a bar of candy for three cents. In case we arrived to the girlfriend's house during mealtime, we would sit in another room while she ate, or she refused to eat until the date was over.

The only light was kerosene, and often we had to sit in the dark when someone in the household had to use it in search for something in another room. This was when smooching took place. It was not always possible to run with the fellows who had automobiles, so you were forced to foot it out. Many times I was glad to kiss my date goodnight, that is if her parents were far enough in front, on the way home, or behind. And of course, being dark you kiss her quickly without being seen. But don't let her parents go into the house before you said goodnight, else you might get more than a kiss as some parents were impressed with their daughter's dates and in fact urged them to get married.

This was encouraged in many ways, but for God's sake don't let her come up pregnant. Even if you were not the guilty one or victim of the situation, you were held to be liable. This was what we commonly called the "shot-gun wedding." I never knew anyone to get shot, but to make sure this didn't occur, the couple got married even though they had nothing but each other. Different ones in the community gave certain items such as odds and ends in silver, a chair here and there, and nothing matched. Salmon cans were used for drinking cups, nail kegs were used to sit on. I was at a disadvantage with girls my age because I was not allowed to be caught out with the girls as early as many of my friends. I had to sneak out with my girls, and it came a time when they wanted their boy friends to go out with them with other couples.

I longed for the day to come when I could wear long pants instead of knee-high pants and accept dates with the girls like my peer group was allowed to do in our community and keep late hours at night as well as smoke cigarettes. I was not allowed to wear long pants until mid-teenage, while others were allowed to wear long pants at an earlier age. I also had to wear long underwear (LFD's) while others wore BVD's, as we called them. When I left home for church or other social occasions, I had my long draws (down in my stockings). We always had to be on guard when our parents were around; many others also wore long underwear, but with long pants on, it was not noticeable.

My first long pants suit was given to me by a cousin from Toledo, Ohio, and I was afraid Dad was not going to allow me to wear it. But he did. Most of our clothing and shoes were ordered from Sears Roebuck, and you measured your feet, in case of shoes being ordered. And mind you, it took from two to three weeks for the order to come, and when you went to the post office to find that the order had been shipped you could expect it to arrive four or five days afterward. And sometimes, in case of shoes, they were too small, but one would refuse to return them for a larger size as it took so long to go through this procedure. Many times when I walked to my girl friend's home, approximately a mile, I had to go the same distance in the opposite direction back home. And the minute I got out of sight, I pulled my shoes off and walked barefoot. If I heard someone coming (on a cloudy night one could not see but heard the approaching individual) I would sit and put the shoes on immediately. As soon as they were out of sight, I pulled them off immediately. By this time of night you were hungry since you had nothing to eat since breakfast except the candy bar and soft drink. We were familiar with every orchard or watermelon in the area, and in case they were not too far off from the way home, we went by and paid them a visit. Speaking of shoes too small, we sometimes got a friend to break them in. This perhaps accounted for many of those who had bad feet back in those days. We were not allowed to wear slippers, or low quarters during winter, but high tops instead, and it was seldom one had shoes other than black in color. I lost quite a few girls because I was not allowed to stay out after a certain time at night with the gang.

When I look back at my peer group of those days, the majority of them are deceased. Those who are still living, I see every once in a while, but they don't know the value of having a family physician or a dentist. Some don't have teeth, or those they have are doing more harm to the body than good. They're chewing tobacco and dipping snuff and never own a tooth brush. We lived among them for a few years until we saw fit to move out.

We took a bath once a week, Saturday night, in the wash tub behind the stove. We were always aware that the side of the tub next to the stove was always hot; and therefore, were reminded when we unconsciously touched the hot side. After the so-called bath, we dried on the underwear which had been worn during the week. Each one used a kettle of hot water, while one took his bath, an additional kettle was being heated for the next one. We bathed in the order in which we voted. Whoever said, "I'm first!" was first, and those who said, "I'm second," etc. came in that order. Each child had certain chores, such as taking care of the livestock, gathering the eggs, bringing in wood, water and slop jars, or chambers, etc. Chores were assigned on a day-to-day basis, and in case one neglected his or her assignment until after dark they were punished by having to go out in the dark to do the assignment. The girls were afraid to go out alone after dark. We inherited a bathroom set, chamber, slopjar, pitcher, and soap dish when we moved into our new home. In order to display these items, I had a washstand made by the Pierce Furniture Co., where we purchased the three piece bedroom suite and two night tables for the master bedroom.

My mind goes back to days when we had a slopjar or two, and there were times when we used a regular gallon bucket for the boy's room. Someone from the rooms was responsible for emptying these the next morning. It was an honor, when one was sick, to have someone else to empty your jar the next day. The slop jars had tops (so did the chambers), but in case it became necessary to use a bucket, the improvised top didn't always keep the odors from escaping, especially where it was a case of excretion. But this was a common practice at that time.

Chewing gum was a rarity that we seldom enjoyed, however, there were certain trees in our community that produced a gum-like substance we called sweet-gum. This substance grew on the bark of the tree, somewhat like bees wax, but clear in color. I don't remember the season of the year when this substance was produced, but we always looked forward to the day when it was available so that we could have something to chew. It took experience to knead it, otherwise it would stick to your teeth and was difficult to remove. Mother did most of the kneading until we learned how to do our own. I can't explain just how she did it, but after having chewed it for a few minutes it was ready, and she passed it out to each of us. We'd have a ball; when we got tired of chewing, each of us had a certain place to stick it until the next time. We used such places as nail heads on the wall as well as window and door frames. Sometimes we had to fan flies off in order to get it when time came for us to chew again. Our screens were not always sufficient enough to keep flies out; we also had cats, but we still had mice in the house at times. One of Dad's sisters, who lived nearby in Mississippi, went to bed one night and kept feeling something cold at her feet under the cover. Finally, she discovered that it was moving occasionally, and when she finally got out of the bed and pulled the cover off, there was a snake in bed with her.

We knew nothing about pasteurization of milk. We milked the cows, and Mother placed the milk in a jar until which time cream, as she called it "rose," accumulated on the top of the milk after which we churned the milk until the cream became butter. Our family meal, many times, consisted of hot biscuits, a glass of milk, and butter stirred into sorghum molasses. All was grown on the farm except the biscuits, and very seldom did one have to visit the doctor's office or hospital. Unless we as children were very sick, we didn't tell our parents because they believed that castor oil the cure for most illnesses. And back in those

22

days, it had no taste, and was thick and slimy and we dared to not swallow it because in case we didn't, we had to take it again. In case we did not admit that we were ill, Mother said she could tell when we had a temperature by feeling our forehead with the back of her hand. This was similar to a thermometer, and in the meantime she looked you in the eyes. In case they were red or not normal, you were sick, and we knew what was next -- castor oil! In case of pain in any part of the body, she applied what she called a mustard plaster to the pain and caused the pain to vanish. You might smell like a goat in the garlic patch, but you were relieved of the pain. Early in the spring, we were given what they called, "three sixes (666)" to clean you out. These remedies helped, but nothing takes the place of seeing the doctor every once in a while. I can see why one who reached the age of fifty or sixty years old and seldom lived beyond that age. Eyeglasses were unknown. When one got to the point he couldn't read (while some never learned to read), it was too bad. There were those who purchased eyeglasses as a part of their attirement, even though they were detrimental to the eye from a physical point of view. Many children who needed eyeglasses either failed in school or just plain dropped out because they needed glasses. During rainy season when it was necessary to wear boots, we could never wear them in the house because they were never clean enough to wear inside. We cleaned them fairly good by scraping the mud off on the edge of the porch and on the posts, and sometimes mud was approximately a foot high on the posts. After which they were pulled off on the bootjack, which was homemade from a board approximately eighteen inches long. It was one inch thick in diameter with a "V" shape in one end which was mounted on a board about the width of the board in order to elevate the "V" to pull the boot off at the end of the day. This same method was used when it became necessary to wear boots to school, except we generally wore our boots throughout the day at school. As we grew up, in an effort to attract the opposite sex, we carried our shoes to school and put them on and left the boots outside until time to go home. In case of foul weather, they were kept in the back of the school.

Sometimes the weather was so bad we rode mules, double-back, two on a mule. And just like we took our lunch in a bucket, we carried corn for the mules and fed them at lunch time as we ate. We lived approximately three quarters of a mile from school. We had no school buildings *per se*; all classes were held in the

23

church, and one teacher taught all classes from kindergarten through the eighth grade. She/he sometimes found it necessary to appoint an upperclassman to complete all classes by the end of the day. We only had classes four and one half days per week.

Friday afternoon was set aside for programs, such as spelling (bee) matches, public speeches, or baseball games. This was all voluntary; the best speller was always identified at the head of the class. Sometimes several students missed the word as it went down the line, but finally it was spelled, and the speller went to the head of the line. There was no special preparation made for the speaking contest. We never knew just what to expect during the speeches. For example, one fellow's speech went like this:

All I want is God's creation, a pretty little wife and a big plantation. All it takes to make me happy is two little children to call me pappy--one named Sop, the other named Gravy, and the next one I get, we'll name him David.

The ballgames or teams were made up from among students in our own school. Ever so often we were either invited to other schools to play, or they came to us. We didn't know what it was like to purchase a new text book. They were handed down from those who had finished that particular grade; sometimes there were missing pages, but we got by somehow. Report cards were unheard of. Students automatically passed to the next grade the next year. 4-H clubs were very popular in Mississippi during our time. I won the public speaking contest on the local level, but lost in the state at-large. I also had the best twelve ears of field corn on exhibit at another time. This won me a trip to the Memphis (Tenn.) Tri-State Fair. To me this was like a trip to the World's Fair.

As a result of the poor educational system, many poor, innocent kids have been doomed to failure. Discipline was very strict, not only in the home, but at school as well. Teachers always felt free to discipline students without fear of what parents thought. In fact, if we were punished at school for certain acts, our parents wanted to know what it was all about so that it would be determined as to whether it was necessary for a repeat performance at home. Most schools were

24

located near wooded areas where switches were always accessible, and teachers always kept a full supply of all sizes for their convenience. When lashes were given, it was always understood that they were not given over jackets and other wraps. Teachers sometimes required that one stood on one foot, out where everyone could see, for a given period of time; and in case the other foot was placed on the floor before the time expired, the punishment was either extended or the punishment took some further proceeding.

We always looked forward to the daily devotion in the school where all classes came together for a period of thirty or forty minutes and sang hymns, had Bible reading and prayers, and many times guest ministers or some other public-spirited citizens came in and lectured. The heating system in the school was usually a pot-bellied stove, which served the school and the church. The wood for school was supplied by the public-spirited citizens in the community. Usually there was a janitor who took care of the heat and cleanliness for the church, but students took care of the heat during the time when school was in session. The teachers assigned different ones to be responsible for the heat and required them to get to school around an hour early in order to see that the building was reasonably warm by school time.

There were nails around the walls of the church (usually in the rear) for those who wore wraps and brought their lunch (usually in buckets) to be kept on until recess at which time certain students were assigned to pass these to who they belonged. By the same token, there were those who were appointed each day before school closed to clean the building for the next day. At noon-time children of each family ate together; the food was in a bucket, and the number in the family determined the size of the bucket. There were no tables or chairs provided for those who ate. In case of unfavorable weather, we ate in the school-room. I recall at one time there was a male teacher who felt the need to teach or emphasize courtesy between boys and girls. He placed special emphasis on the importance of boys' cleaning mud off the girls' feet before entering the school room and carrying the girls' books on the way home, in case they were going in the same direction. We had one male teacher who liked baseball and participated in the game. We liked him because sometimes when the game was interesting, our noon hour was extended. These and other fallacies caused our parents much concern about the future of the educational system in that area.

They felt the need to expose us to a better environment in which to worship and be educated. They made arrangements with relatives in other areas to allow us to go to schools where the schools were better. The family was too big to send everyone away to school. Since I was the older, they sent me to Clarksdale, Mississippi one year to go to school and live with one of Dad's sisters. Because I had spent a year in Jackson, Tennessee two years prior to this time, I enjoyed this experience much better and had a broader concept of the difference in the school systems. In 1925 Aunt Ella, whom I lived with in Clarksdale, moved to Gulf Port, Mississippi. Since I had done so well in Clarksdale, they decided to send me to Gulf Port for a year.

This is where I learned to eat raw oysters and drink moonshine. At that time Gulf Port was dry, and I never saw so many bootleggers in all of my life. Aunt Ella and Uncle James Brown bought it by the gallons. They never hid it from me. Whenever the time came for them to replenish it, they always took me with them. They were always given a free drink at the time of the purchase, and they always offered me a drink. However, Aunt Ella always hastened to say, "No thanks" for me. When Mother used to bake tea cakes at home, she always hid them until time for the family to eat together. In order to get a few extras, I decided to watch where she hid them and this worked out pretty good. This scheme, when I decided to try the moonshine, also worked. They worked six days per week, and I was in school only five days. Therefore, I slept late on Saturday morning in order to let them get off to work. The minute they took off to work I got my share of moonshine, as I knew where they hid it in the closet. For fear I couldn't destroy the odor in a glass, I'd turn the jug up and drink from it. In that way I didn't know just how much to drink; therefore, they came home a few times thinking I was asleep and I was drunk. I enjoyed my stay in Gulf Port better than at Jackson, Tennessee or Clarksdale, Mississippi.

From childhood up to that point I saw too many who could not afford a car that one could depend on to get any place, not only motor-wise, but the tires and tubes were not too reliable. Every once in a while it was noted that someone in the community bought a secondhand car that was just about worn out and could not be depended on to run. Also they always carried a container in order to replenish water in the radiator. They were familiar with every pond along the way in order to refill the leaky radiator. It was common to see such cars stranded along the wayside, in need of repair or stuck in the mud, during the rainy season. Sometimes it was two or three days before they were moved. Wreckers were unknown; said cars were moved by hitching mules or horses to them in order to pull them to the desired point. Gasoline was only fifteen or twenty cents per gallon, and I could not afford that, even a quarter on the gas bill.

I noticed through my high school career that the fellow who owned an automobile seldom had to walk in case his automobile was unavailable because his friends, who owned automobiles, always welcomed him to ride with them. Even though I did not own an automobile, many of those friends with cars always welcomed me. They said that I always knew how to gain the girls' attention. I was known as the jive man; I always seemed to have what it took in order to approach the girls, not in looks however. I learned to drive an automobile while in Gulf Port. In Gulf Port there were many places to go and much scenery between Gulf Port and Biloxi. The Browns never hesitated to allow me the use of the car because I always returned on schedule. I was quite lucky on one occasion; I came to a curve too deep to make at a rapid speed but was successful even though (I think) I turned it on two wheels. Back in those days, official driver training was unheard of, or unknown. Of course, one learned on his own with the assistance of a relative or friend. Those who owned automobiles in the community could almost be counted on one hand. If the car owner lived in the rural area, he enjoyed his car during the summer. When winter weather came he might as well drive his car into the garage, if he owned one, and forget it until spring. It was not uncommon to find one's car stuck in the mud when he thought he could make the trip to no avail. He had only one choice to move it, and that was to go home and harness his team so perhaps it could be moved with the combination of team and the motor. At times a shovel was used to make a trench to get the car started moving. Sometimes such cars were left for two or three days before the owner moved them. I recall a time when Mother's younger sister visited us, on Squirrel Lake, in her car which she allowed me to drive. But each time I did something wrong which caused the motor to become locked; therefore, I didn't get very far with my effort. With the Gulf Port experience I obtained a driver's license in 1940, here in Frankfort, Kentucky.

I wanted to stay in Gulf Port during summer vacation from school, but was forced to go back home to work on the farm since while I was in school in Gulf Port, Mississippi, the family had moved to Cold Water River, approximately three miles west of Darling. This move took place in the fall of 1926. Dad had told me that he would either buy a car or move that year. And of course I though he'd buy the car as he was always on the road, but he didn't. This proved to be the worst few years of our life before leaving Mississippi. The soil was much depleted of its fertility. Therefore, the crops were poor, and the schools were similar to those which we left behind on Squirrel Lake. In fact, we were unfortunate to run into a former man teacher who once taught on Squirrel Lake. His social life seemed to have taken precedence over his teaching. He dated a young lady in the community whose family seemed to have always had the last word. I was disappointed with the move. This proved to be the worse move that could have been made at that time. The land was poor and the dwelling in which we lived was too small to accommodate the family. There was no porch where one coming into the house from the outside could condition his feet before entering the house during winter. I became acquainted with the efficiency type dwelling, where the dining area was a part of the kitchen or living area, but this was the first time we were forced to eat and sleep in the same room. The bed was located near the table where two or three could use the side of the bed instead of chairs at mealtime.

Willie M., the half brother, was in Alcorn College at this time, but he knew what was going on and reiterated his previous opinion that Dad probably should have stayed on Squirrel Lake. He, with our parents' consent, made arrangements for me to come with him to Alcorn, work a year, and enter school there the second year. This was the happiest moment of my life. He sent me a one way ticket to Alcorn. And when I arrived to Alcorn, he met me at the bus station and took me to his room where we sat while he told me about the plan for me. He had arranged for me to stay in his room with him and two other college students. My job was to work in the faculty cafeteria. This was the most promising opportunity of my life as an eight grader. The association was so rich; I attended most activities on the campus, and every day I looked forward to the day when I too would be enrolled

28

in class at Alcorn; in spite of the fact that I was only in the eighth grade. I found myself a girlfriend who was in the freshman class. She accepted me; I was older than she, but even as an eighth grader we had quite a bit in common.

Our parents stayed on the farm, on Cold Water River, one more year. After that they became so discouraged with the situation there they decided to move, this time to Jonestown, Mississippi. Not only were the schools better, but the location in general was superb. There were four or five teachers on the faculty, and all were much better qualified than any we had ever had. This was the first school we ever attended where there was a piano. Right after this move, Dad became ill and could not take care of the duties on the farm. As a sharecropper and being his first year on a plantation, it became obvious that either Willie M. or I had to answer the call to duty at home to substitute for Dad. Even though Willie M. and I were away in school, one of the two had to go home in order to assume this role. I had been in Alcorn only seven months working, not enrolled as a student, but had high hopes of starting school the following September. Willie M. was a junior. He and I decided that I should go since it was time to prepare the farm for that year's crop, March 1929. We felt that this was only temporary and that Dad would be able to resume his role by the following September so I could return to Alcorn then. Mrs. U. J. Wade Foster was in charge of my job and agreed to re-admit me in September on a part-time basis so that I could enroll in school. This was the year the family moved to Jonestown, Mississippi on another plantation.

When a family moved on a plantation, in Mississippi, it was not the head of the house's decision as to how many in the family was of working age; child labor law meant nothing, and the wife was also counted as a part of the work-force. She prepared three meals each day and worked along with the rest of the family on the farm. As the children became old enough to supply the family with water as they worked, this was their job. And when they became eight or ten years of age, they were expected to work along with the rest of the family, under close supervision. I was very much excited when I came to Jonestown because this was a much better community as far as convenience was concerned. It was a four room log-house on the gravel road just outside the city limit where we could sit on the porch and see the cars drive by. The paperboy came by throwing the Memphis daily paper) on our porch. We had a mail box at the Post Office where we could pick up our mail daily and walk to school and church, less than a half mile from home. Boots were no longer needed to wear to church, school, or social affairs; they were only needed by those who worked on the farm during winter weather.

It was not uncommon for teenage boys and girls to be in the eighth grade on Squirrel Lake or Coldwater River because work on the farm took priority over school especially for boys. They were expected to help with the heavy work, such as breaking the ground in preparation for the next crop in the new year or cutting and hauling hay and the winter wood. This was most embarrassing to me because the people in the community had learned that Rev. Simmons' son was dropping out of college to take his place on the farm on a temporary basis until Rev. Simmons was able to take over. I was aware of the fact that it was impossible to misrepresent my status to people in the new community by telling them that I was fifteen years of age and was a full time employee in the cafeteria with high hopes of entering the eighth grade the following September. It was also hard for me to become oriented into the new system of farming. On Squirrel Lake, where much of the land was not cultivated, we grazed our livestock wherever the grass was the greenest without being questioned. The cows were chained with a chain approximately twenty five or thirty feet long and moved from one place to another as they ate to the length of the chain. In some situations where they became tangled to a nearby object before having eaten the grass, they were untangled to expose them to the rest of the grass before moving them to a new location. In case it was too wet to work on the farm or the farm work was cultivated up to par, we grazed the mules by sitting on them while they ate. This was a means of keeping them from eating the cultivated crops. Pastures were not too plentiful in that area. A few farmers fenced in certain areas and called it "the pasture," but there were more trees than grass in said areas. When I went to Jonestown, I found farming on a plantation was all together different; the landlord told his tenants what they could or could not grow. We were permitted to have a vegetable garden and a pig and chicken or two, and that was IT. The landlord had a central location where his mules and horses were kept under the supervision of what they called "a horselar." His job was to maintain these animals and issue them to the tenant farmers as the need arose. In case one lived a certain distance from the central location, he was permitted to keep said animals at his house during the noon hour and feed them there in order to expedite the time. The horselar also worked around the landlord's house when called upon to serve meals, and to tell the landlord what he wanted to know about families or individuals. I stayed there two years while Dad recuperated.

As time passed, things grew progressively worse relative to my plans to return to Alcorn. It seemed that the harder I worked, the darker the future looked for me. Many times I worked at the oil mill unloading cotton seeds from a railroad box car for five dollars a carload. There was a man in the community who drove a dray wagon, a strong, heavy vehicle low for convenience in loading heavy articles, drawn by two mules. This man saw I was in desperate need for money to go to school. He suggested that when I ran out of work or it rained where I could not work on the farm, to report to him and he would help me. This thrilled me to no end; the first time I reported to him for work he suggested that I go to the office and ask his boss for a seed fork so that we could haul cotton seeds that day. When I went into the office and asked for a seed fork, I told him that Mr. Johnson said we'd haul cotton seeds that day. He asked me, "Who is Mr. Johnson?" I said, "Mr. Harry Johnson, the man who works for you." He said there's not such as "Mr. Nigger." I wanted to kill him so bad. We had the gun. All I needed was a supply of ammunition because I wanted to kill as many whites, him first, and as many others as possible before killing myself. It took me two or three months to get over this ordeal. I finally decided that it wouldn't pay. In case I succeeded with this plan, there were my parents, five sisters, and one brother to suffer the consequences. And in case I didn't succeed in killing myself, perhaps they'd handcuff me, put a chain around my neck attach it to a vehicle, saturate me with gasoline, set me on fire, and drag me through the Black neighborhood while telling them that this is what a smart nigger gets. I'm so thankful to God that this didn't tarnish my attitude toward my fellowman regardless to race, color, or creed.

Dad tried to always keep a written record when it came to finances. Near the end of the cotton picking season when he felt that daylight was near, he compared figures with the landlord. He felt that so many bales of cotton should put him out of debt, and the rest was his. On one occasion it was found that the landlord's book didn't balance, and he challenged the landlord who resented him questioning his record and expressed it in that like-manner. Dad, who had a pretty good knowledge of the Bible, told him that a man could ask a favor in hell.

When there was no more cotton to be picked, I began searching for work in other areas. I can't recall just how I found out that the railroad company was hiring new employees in Cohoma County, not too far from Clarksdale, Mississippi. I hitch-hiked to said area and was hired. This was a better paying job than I'd ever had. But the environment was unbearable; men, all black, except the foreman, lived like lower animals. And they were treated like lower animals; we slept in tents with no facility and no water. Body eliminations were carried out behind trees. The heat from the sun and also the mosquitoes were unbearable. Sears Roebuck catalogue, corn cobs and leaves, from bushes in the woods, were substitutes for toilet paper, depending on the location of the individual at the appropriate time. It was obvious that these men had no home training and very little respect for each other. And they were treated like they were not human. I stayed only one week, after which I told the boss that I could not stay any longer. When he paid me, I took off for home with no regrets. My parents were surprised that I could not do the job, but they agreed when I told them about the situation.

During WPA days before we left Mississippi, things got so tough I had no choice but to apply for a job on the WPA. I found myself working for the WPA as a last resort. This was a far cry from the job on the railroad, but the atmosphere was so much better. I went from one extreme to another. The pay was meager, and so was the work. One of my first assignments was to help patch the sidewalk in front of my girl friend's house. When I reported for work along with others, the boss who was always white, explained what type of work we would be doing, such as patching places in the streets and side walks. Immediately it came to mind that there was a broken place on the sidewalk in front of my girl friend's house, and I was sure this would be one of our jobs and that I'd be one of the crew to do the job. Sure enough, it happened just as I expected. It was commonly known just who was on welfare, and most blacks and poor whites were the subjects. But when it came to working the streets and sidewalks, it was below our dignity, but we had to eat. There was a joke at that time about welfare workers (WPA): "If it doesn't move, don't shoot, it might be a WPA worker." I was a bit reluctant in visiting my girl friend when she found that I was working on the WPA, but she

32

was quite understanding; in fact, she was more understanding than I was. It took me quite sometime to realize that welfare work was not so bad after all if one had no other source of income.

I often thought about the situation when it was all over; it would have been much better being caught working on the WPA than stealing a white man's plow. Yet the white landowners owned hundreds of acres of land, and they forced the share cropper to purchase food and clothing of the cheapest quality for an unusually high price. They furnished flour by the Red Cross with labels which read, "Not to be Sold" to the share cropper for a fee, but if it got back to the Federal Government, the landowner would be punished.

Outhouses were very popular during those days. The outhouse was a small building about 4' x 6' in size and approximately six feet tall. The stool was approximately two feet tall and was covered with a two by twelve inch board with two or three holes about eight or ten inches in diameter to sit on. Many times there were spaces in the rear large enough for chickens to feed from the feces; lime was sometimes used to keep flies away. Instead of doors, a sack or some form of cloth was used as a substitute. In late years, we learned to dig a pit underneath the stool, but the handicap there was that during unusually rainy seasons these pits were filled with water which created an additional problem.

I suppose I was in my late teens when I became acquainted with bathrooms on a day-to-day basis. In fact, I felt out of place for a long time before I realized that the stool was to be used in the house. We were accustomed to going out in the backyard to the outhouse. In fact, on many occasions we just stepped around to the back of the house or a nearby tree to eliminate our kidney, or urinate. To bring in the slop jar before bedtime was always assigned to one on a nightly or weekly basis. If those who were given this assignment forgot to carry it out before dark, our parents insisted that they do it alone in the dark even though they feared darkness. In case one was too sick to go to the outhouse, he used the slop jar at night, and someone else was assigned to carry it out and see that the jar was clean before bringing it back into the house. This was quite a treat for the sick, especially during bad weather, because the slop jar was to have been used only by those who were unable to go to the outhouse.

Unless one was very ill, it was not commonly known by Mother because she believed in castor oil, and back in those days the taste was quite unpleasant. Mother could always tell when any of the children were not feeling well; she would look you over while talking and finally feel your forehead with the back of her hand which indicated you had fever in many cases. You might as well prepare to take a big dose of castor oil; and if you vomited or threw up, you had a repeat performance. Some of Mother's home remedies for external skin rashes, etc. caused one to smell like a goat in the garlic patch, but results were obtained. Mother used many home remedies, and they worked. In order to get the doctor (and there was only one in Darling, Mississippi three miles away) one had to ride a mule to the doctor's office to find him away from his office visiting patients in other areas. He too had to go on horseback in order to reach patients when the roads were bad.

I felt it an honor when I became janitor of the church in my early teens. This job consisted of preparing the church for regular Sunday services, seeing that the building was clean, building a fire during winter months, and ringing the bell (a big bell mounted approximately ten or fifteen feet above ground level). The bell had a rope attached which extended below so that it could be reached from the ground. It was the janitor's job to ring the bell at 9:30 Sunday mornings for Sunday school, 11:00 or 12:00 for morning worship, and when one passed away.

Undertakers, *per se*, were unknown. Friends helped to prepare the body for burial. Embalming was unheard of; the body was cleaned and dressed, and a white band (about two or three inches wide and long enough to be placed under the chin extending around the chin) was pulled together over the head in order to keep the mouth closed. In order to close the eyes a coin was placed over each eyelid. The casket had to be brought from ten miles away in Marks, Mississippi. It was crudely put together, often referred to as a "tooth-pick." The persons delivering the casket placed the body in and departed. The body was placed in the wagon, in the center of the wagon bed, so that the family and friends could sit on either side of the casket in route to the cemetery which was located near the church. As the funeral procession approached the church, the janitor would toll the bell.

34

Many ministers back in those days used a different approach from today's ministers with regards to consoling the family in the time of bereavement. For example, I recall on one occasion a minister, during his discourse, appealed to the congregation by saying, "John Doe don't have no wife, and chil'in don't have no mamie!" After the sermon, the body was placed in the wagon, in case the grave was not located close to the church where it could be carried to the grave by the casket bearers. Upon arrival to the grave, the casket was taken to the grave by six men, three on either side, with poles, long slender pieces of wood about six feet long placed over the grave on two or three similar poles until time for the casket to be lowered in the grave. This was done by taking the wagon lines and placing them under the casket with at least four men, depending on the size body. Two additional poles were placed below the casket so that the lines could be withdrawn before the grave was covered. Hymns were sung while the grave was being covered by volunteers. Graves were also dug by volunteers.

We always conserved rain water by placing a barrel under the gutter as Mother thought this was the best water to wash clothes with. Wallpaper was unknown back in those days; walls were papered with newspapers, if available. We knew nothing about the daily, or even weekly, newspaper. Pages from old Sears Roebuck or Montgomery Ward catalogues were used. Mother made the paste to hang whatever paper was used. We spent much time looking at the attractions from papers on the wall while cracking hickory nuts, popping pop corn or roasting peanuts to eat, especially at night as there was nothing else to do. Mother suggested that I read sometimes instead of being on the go. There was nothing else to read except the Bible and Sunday School lesson. We purchased quite a bit of our clothing from Sears Roebuck and Montgomery Ward; it was not uncommon for a garment or a pair of shoes not to fit, but we usually kept them. I recall a pair of shoes being a bit too small for me, but I failed to let my parents know this because I was too anxious to wear them after having waited two or three weeks for them to come. In one case I had a friend whose feet were a size smaller; he'd share the misery by wearing mine in an effort to "break them in." I've walked home many a night, two or three miles, with my shoes in my hand because they were uncomfortable. If someone was approaching, I would put them on quickly until they passed. This might have been the cause for corns on my feet until I was in my late teens.

I am also reminded of many nights when a group of us teens was returning home from an event hungry and saw a farmer's watermelon patch or orchard conveniently located, especially at harvest time. We took advantage of the opportunity to satisfy our hunger. In case no one had a knife, we burst a watermelon with our fists. If it didn't suit our taste, we kept searching until the right one was found.

We always looked forward to Thanksgiving and Christmas. On Thanksgiving Day we had all kinds of food, such as turkey, country ham, and two or three vegetables as well as two or three kinds of cakes and pies. In addition to the extra foods at Christmas, we looked forward to receiving fruit, candy, and a few fireworks. Fruit and candy tasted better at Christmas than any other time of the year because Santy Clause brought them. We were always told that we had to go to bed early and go to sleep, or Old Santy would put ashes in our eyes and give our Christmas to someone else. Most all of our toys were homemade such as stitch, made from poles about one and one half inches in diameter about five or six feet long with stirrups attached approximately two feet from the bottom as an inverted U-shaped piece of metal or wood with flat foot-pieces suspended, commonly called "tom walkers." We also made a toy from the metal rim off the hub from a wagon wheel. We took a board approximately two inches wide and two feet long, trimmed one end as a handle and attached a portion of a barrel hoop to the other end in order to guide the wheel in the desired direction. The rate of speed depended on the individual whether he wanted to walk or run. Nearby neighbors always gave us a special gift on New Year's Day; they called it a gift from Santa Claus' wife "Christina."

One of the biggest mistakes I ever made was when I failed to take music (piano) lessons. It only cost twenty-five cents per lesson. I started out in a big way and enjoyed it until the boys started teasing me by saying such things as only "ponks" took music. I had to ride a mule to the teacher's house as she lived approximately two miles away. I learned the keyboard well enough to play for my sister who sang a solo during a convention. Music speaks all languages to all peoples.

Less than six months after I came to Jonestown, I could see clearly that my chances for returning to Alcorn were bleak. When we harvested our crop, apparently we broke even with the landlord; therefore, we had to pick cotton for others in order to survive through the winter. Occasionally I was able to find odd jobs, but with that we were not able to purchase all necessities for survival. Dad had a niece who lived on South Lake, and she and her husband owned their farm. They had no children. While visiting with them on one occasion, I told them about my plight, and they immediately agreed to allow me to farm three acres of their land, without charge. They also allowed me the use of their mules and farming tools free. I agreed to work for them, between times, when my cotton was cultivated up to par or free of weeds and grass. They also allowed me to grow sorghum for molasses and a sweet potato patch for our family, as the landlord did not permit these crops to be grown on his plantation. I was very happy over this proposed agreement, but was not sure as to how my parents would feel about the deal. When I went home and discussed the proposed plan with them, they accepted it without reservations, and said the family would make plans to help pick the cotton free of charge.

I had a friend in Jonestown who wanted to know if he could get in on the deal; I promised him that I'd take it up with my cousin as soon as possible and get back with him soon. The following week, I went back to South Lake to tell them that my parents had OK'd our plans, and they would make plans to help pick my cotton free of charge. I also told them about my friend from Jonestown who had expressed interest in a similar arrangement, if possible. His name was John Morris. He immediately took this situation up with his cousin who agreed to give John a similar proposition. Within a week's time, John and I went to South Lake to Mr. White's house, and they too got together on a similar deal as mine, except he was not interested in growing sorghum and sweet potatoes. In fact, John did not have anyone to turn to in order to pick the cotton; he had only two sisters, and they knew nothing about farming and could care less. John did not know anything about farming, but he depended on me as a guide. Our friendship grew out of our dating two girls, Mamie Rias and Zuma Sanders, who were close friends and lived next door to each other in Jonestown. During the first of March, 1928, John and I took off for South Lake in order to break the ground for our cotton crop for that year. This was John's first experience as a farmer, but he was eager to learn and did a beautiful job under Mr. White's supervision. He and I both were overly excited because this was our first experience to be on our own, and as youngsters we felt that we would make a barrel of money that year.   Our Jonestown friends were misled as a result of what we told them. It was impossible for us to go home every weekend during the months of March, April and May because of our farming program, and we had no money or transportation for which to make the trip between South Lake and Jonestown which were approximately twenty-five miles apart. We tried to visit our girl friends at least every two weeks. We didn't live together as *per se*; he roomed with his landlord, and I roomed with my cousin, rent free.

I recall one weekend we became homesick and decided to visit our girlfriends, even if it was for just an hour. We left South Lake, after dark, one night walking, hoping to hitchhike a ride to no avail. We walked all night, taking a break every five or six miles. Talking about walking in my sleep -- I slept in my walking. Some of our best friends lived outside the city limits of Jonestown near the road which we had to travel, and we did not want them to see us walking into town; therefore, we had to walk faster than we would otherwise because they were of the opinion that we were better off money-wise than we really were. We were there all day Saturday and until mid-afternoon Sunday. We felt that our chances for catching a ride were much better during the daylight hours. We got back to South Lake before midnight; our morals were lifted very high during the week.

After crops were laid by, during the months of July and mid August, we spent most of this time in Jonestown. Our peer group looked up to us because we were venturing out on our own, which was unusual for boys our ages, even if they had an opportunity such as we. I had to return to South Lake about two weeks before cotton-picking time in order to process the sorghum which I grew for my immediate family. The family joined me as was originally planned; we processed the sorghum and hauled it to the mill the same day. When our turn came to make the molasses it only took three of us to do the job. We thought everything was in proper order and proceeded to grind the juice from the stalks into the fifty-five gallon barrel which was sunken about two thirds beneath the surface of the ground. We failed to check the barrel prior to completion of the job because we

38

knew the barrel would not be filled with the amount of sorghum we had. When the job was completed and we thought we were ready to transfer the juice to the cooking pan, the barrel was opened to find it was empty. It had holes all around beneath the ground surface; therefore, all of our hopes and aspirations had been absorbed into the ground. When the cotton was ready to be picked, the family was unable to help with the harvest, free of charge, because they needed the money for survival during the winter. Therefore, I had to pay local people to pick the cotton because extra expenses would have involved transportation and others, such as food, etc. When the job was completed, I only cleared enough money to buy a cheap suit of clothes, a pair of fortune shoes which cost $4.00, and five bushels of sweet potatoes which I grew for the family.

I ordered my suit from Great Western Tailoring Co. in Chicago, Illinois. I received samples from this company in order to eliminate the middleman, and later I became one of their salesmen. When the suit arrived at the post office, I was short of six or seven dollars for which to get it from the post office. Mother and I tried every way possible to get it out by Sunday,. and she finally borrowed the money from one of her church organizations, so that I could have my suit to wear Sunday. I made a special trip to the postman's house that Sunday morning, and he kindly went to the post office and let me have it to wear that Sunday, and was I glad.

This is when I became desperate. I decided to go either to school or jail. At this time I was seventeen years old and decided that the jail couldn't be much worse than where I was. I decided to steal a plow, a two-mule cultivator, from the plantation owner where my family lived. My cousin, whom I made the crop with, agreed to give me $19.00 for the plow. And the next question that came to mind was: "How am I to get the plow delivered?" I had no money or transportation, but I had a friend who agreed to make the delivery for me. This plow had been left in the field after plowing season was over, and it was conveniently located for removing without attracting attention from passers-by. We had a choice between two routes to take between Jonestown and South Lake; the best route was a gravel road all the way, but it was approximately ten miles longer, and again we would have been exposed to more people. We chose the nearer way, to our regrets.

There were two miles of dirt road on this route, and it had just rained the day before to render it almost impassable, but we figured by being extra cautious we could make it. Evidently we were wrong, however, because we got stuck in less than a mile. At this time, it was around twelve o'clock (midnight), and most people had gone to bed. There was a family that lived nearby whom I knew well, but I was a bit reluctant to tell them about my situation for two reasons: first, we had moved from this community when we went to Jonestown; and second, Dad was the minister who had served this community for one year, and here was his oldest child stealing a plow and getting people out of bed to lend us two mules. They had to be harnessed for us to pull the stolen plow to the end of the dirt road and hide it under a church while we proceeded to free the automobile from the mud. The mules could not do it alone, so we had to walk back to Jonestown, three miles away, in order to get the plow delivered before daylight. Being a bit nervous, we failed to properly hitch the plow to the car; therefore, on the first bridge we attempted to cross, one wheel of the plow hit the guard rail on the bridge and broke the tongue. This left us but one choice, and that was to get rid of the plow in order to not be caught. We placed it under the bridge and never returned to the scene. Thereafter, I crossed that bridge many times, but was afraid to look back for fear someone would identify me as the one who stole the plow.

Now I had to go home and face the family after having been gone all night and returning home looking like a pig muddy from head to toe. But I left the evening before under the assumption that I was going raccoon hunting. I told the family that the dogs treed a raccoon, and we had to cut the tree in order to get him, and he got away as he fought the dog on the way. I thought many times how lucky I was to get out of that situation without having to put up some time in the state prison. Blacks were incarcerated two to one compared to whites who committed the same crime. Whites got preferential treatment under the law while incarcerated, as well as job opportunities when released from prison.

At this time my chances for even going to high school seemed very bleak. A friend in Jonestown was teaching at the Cohoma County High School outside the city limits of Clarksdale and heard about my plight. In talking about my situation, he agreed to let me ride with him to school each day, five days per week, and to pay him later, fifty cents per day. I gladly accepted the offer with no idea as to when or how I would pay him. I commuted with Mr. West Poindexter from mid-September, 1930 until the latter part of November without any knowledge as to when or whether I'd ever be able to pay him.

Mother had a sister who taught school in Southeast Missouri, Concord, just about two miles north of Hayti on Highway #60. She invited her to spend Christmas with her that year and sent Mother a round-trip ticket as a Christmas gift.. This was the answer to our prayers; when Mother and Aunt Priscilla Wesley got through with plans by which she could rent farm land just the size needed for our family and just across Highway #60 from her, we were in business. Mother was a bit reluctant in presenting the proposed plans to Dad because she was not sure he would be willing to leave the state of Mississippi. But it was also music to his ears. I always admired Dad for his philosophy as man being head of the house; in fact, he did the best he could. He was never able to pastor a church large enough to take care of the family needs, and for some reason he never was able to engage in whatever came next as a supplement to the family's needs. 1st Timothy 3-5 reads as follows: "For if a man know not how to rule his own house, how shall he take care of the church of God?" Many times while Dad was away attending revivals, etc., I slept with Mother, and we discussed what should be done in certain matters pertaining to the family affairs, but Dad didn't see it that way. Proverbs 31:10-15. " 10) Who can find a virtuous woman? For her price is far above rubies. 11) The heart of her husband doth safely trust in her, so that he shall have no need of spoil. 12) She will do him good and not evil all the days of her life. 13) She seeketh wool, and flax, and worketh willingly with her hands. 14) She is like the merchants' ships; she bringeth her food from afar. 15) She riseth also while it is yet night, and giveth meat for her household, and a portion to her maidens."

Immediately after Christmas, after Mother and Dad discussed the proposed plans, he called the family together and told us the plan. It came to us children as a surprise; in fact, we the older children had mixed emotions about the proposition. We knew absolutely nothing about Missouri, and no other state and the memories of life's experiences in Mississippi should have automatically inspired us to be willing to make the move. The first thought that came to mind was leaving friends and loved ones behind, especially those of the opposite sex which we had formed close ties with. Economically, however, we realized that we were near the end of the road. After the discussion, Dad notified Aunt "Sid" as she was known by most people who knew her. And she immediately sent a truck down to Mississippi, and we proceeded to pack our belongings and loaded the truck immediately when it arrived. By midnight we were passing though Memphis, Tennessee in route to Hayti, Missouri about one hundred and fifteen miles from Memphis.

During slow times of the year, Dad would hitch the mule to the buggy and go throughout the area, in Mississippi and Southeast Missouri, selling Sayman's products and making pictures. During slow times on the farm for me, I always looked for farm-related work where I could make extra money. I remember, on one occasion, I wanted to give two girls Christmas gifts from Sayman's products: Mamie Rias, in Mississippi and Regina Clifford, in Caruthersville, Missouri. These gifts came ready wrapped for Christmas, for $1.39 each, and had it not been for Mother's sister "Aunt Sweet" as we called her, I would not have been able to pay for them. And mind you, this was wholesale price.

Mother's brother, William Cade, was my favorite uncle. He had two girls and three boys: Rosie, Lillie Mae, William, Charley and Eddie. I always looked for the day when I could spend weekends with Uncle Bud as he was called. Uncle Bud believed that everyone should share responsibilities at home. His philosophy was, "Never engage in a conversation with one who was doing a job without lending a hand." But everybody did his thing, unsupervised. There was no question as to where we went or what time we turned in at night.

After having grown-up, however, I learned the value of law and order at home as well as abroad: until a child reaches the age of maturity, he doesn't realize the importance of law in the home. It prepares one for the law of the land; and it teaches that a sacrifice must be made in order for one to appreciate whatever might come his way. Even though hard to accept, obedience to the law means liberty. It is also said that circumstance alters cases, but I've found it very difficult when one is reared in a family setting where these rules were emphasized on a day to day basis. The family was cemented together with weekly family prayer meetings, Sunday morning family prayer, and periodic family song fests. We had fireside chats, tannings with razor straps, and most of all, parents who loved us and caused us to love each other. When we went to school, these family teachings were continued; and if we were punished at school for a serious charge, we got a repeat when we went home. We were taught to speak to whomever we came in contact with. Mr. J. H. McMillian, Principal of the Rosenwald School in Jonestown, Mississippi, involved himself by personally coaching basketball and baseball, counseling, and inspiring students, large and small. He had the respect of the entire community. Mother said I tried to even walk like him. He was a great public speaker.

After having stayed in Southeast Missouri (1931-1933), I found that the situation for me wasn't getting any better. In fact, it appeared worse than ever before, perhaps because I thought by the time we were there two years I should be able to be released from the family, at age seventeen, and get out on my own, but it just didn't happen that way. This is when I had a heart-to-heart talk with my parents, and they too realized the fact that it was time for a change in my status. I still had in mind to go back to Alcorn, Mississippi. We finally decided that I should go back to Alcorn College, and hopefully they would honor or give me credit for the seven months which I had earned four years ago. I was in dire need of clothing, but was still short of money. Through a friend who lived at Concord, I learned about "pawn shops." And he suggested going to St. Louis, Missouri where there were several to choose from. He was familiar with the city and made frequent visits there. I arranged to go with him on his next visit as I was contemplating going back to Mississippi to enter school in September. He understood that I preferred going on a day when we could return to Southeast Missouri on the same day, as I didn't know anybody in St. Louis and was unable to pay for overnight lodging. I could hardly sleep the night before the trip because in the first place, I had never been to St. Louis, and second, I had permission from Mother and Dad to return to Alcorn.

This was quite a decision to make between leaving the family, when I knew they needed me. And also I had hopes for a family of my own some day, realizing the fact that life or living was becoming more complicated as time passed. And usually the family less qualified to cope with the cost of living had more children. I taught vocational agriculture four years, and one of the questions frequently asked by students, was why farmers seem to have more children than those of other walks of life. My answer was, in bygone years the farmer had nothing to do on the farm during rainy season, so he went to bed and the wife followed. As a result

43

another child was born. But in recent years, the farmer found there were other jobs pertaining to his program that could be done, such as repairing farm equipment or buildings.

I was so excited over the fact that I was to go to St. Louis the next day, I hardly slept the night before. We arrived in St. Louis around midmorning, and I went to two or three pawn shops before making a choice as to what I wanted to purchase. I finally decided to buy a blue pin stripe suit and a pair of pants and a jacket. I don't remember what I paid for the pants and jacket, but the suit cost seven dollars and a half. I do remember I had a dollar or two left out of the twenty dollars I had planned to spend on clothes. When I returned home, everyone seemed excited over my purchase, but I could see a cloud of mixed emotions over the idea that I was preparing to leave the family. I had in mind to hitchhike to Jonestown and to go from there to Alcorn first class. A day before my proposed departure, a cousin came through, driving from Chicago to Mississippi and stopped over-nite with us. We felt that this was an unusual coincidence; he and I agreed that I would help on the trip by contributing to the gas bill. I left thirty dollars with my parents to be forwarded to Jonestown for the trip from there to Alcorn. It's impossible for me to describe how I felt saying goodbye to the family even though I felt that was the time to make my exit.

We left Concord, approximately three miles north of Hayti, Missouri, early in the morning and made good time until we got within a few miles from Memphis, Tennessee. The car started missing. Luckily, we made it to the next filling station, and an attendant at the station did something to it which enabled us to get through Memphis, just inside the state of Mississippi. It stopped completely, and everyone passed us by except a few who stopped to lend a helping hand and failed to get it started. I finally gave up and suggested that I should go to a nearby village in an effort to find someone who could give a helping hand as darkness was near. I feared that in case I took my bag, he would figure I wouldn't return; but he didn't question my departure. I hitchhiked to the next village, which was not too far down Highway 60. I began to inquire about a place to stay overnight, and was fortunate in finding a place. The people were very nice; they gave me dinner and breakfast the next morning. I didn't tell them the whole story; I just told them I was hitchhiking to Jonestown, Mississippi in route to Alcorn College. They wished me well and gave me a lunch to take on the way. When I proceeded to thumbing down the highway, I feared I would run across my cousin again, but luckily, I didn't. I arrived in Jonestown before dark and stopped at Mr. Davis' store and told him about my plan to leave there as soon as my money arrived, which was mailed to him from my parents.

I stayed with the Davises three days. I told them the story about my plan to go to Alcorn, and asked them if they would honor the seven months that I worked there four years ago and give me a job so that I might enter school the following September. Mr. Davis asked if they were expecting me, or if I had discussed my plans with the Alcorn authority prior to this time. And, of course my answer was no; and my reason was that I felt it would be easier for them to turn me down through correspondence than it would be if I were there. He saw the logic in my thinking, but still felt that I was taking a big chance. He told me that his son, Walker, had finished Alcorn and had been hired to teach at Okolona Industrial Junior College, Okolona, Mississippi, and he suggested that I allow him to call Walker and see if they would give me a job to work my way through school. This made sense to me. He called Walker, and within twenty-four hours I was accepted at Okolona Industrial Junior College, Okolona, Mississippi. When my money arrived, I hitchhiked back to Memphis, Tennessee, sixty-nine miles, and from there to Okolona Industrial Junior College, which is one hundred and seven miles from Memphis, Tennessee. It could have been further back in 1932, since highways have been changed considerably which makes it nearer between points today.

When I arrived at the school, Mr. Davis was expecting me and gave me a hearty welcome. He told me that plans had not been completed for me as I was being considered at the last moment. I was given a room in a dormitory, but boarded off the campus with three other students and Mr. Davis. We bought our own groceries and paid a lady, Mrs. Floyd, to prepare two meals per day for us in her home. Perhaps I was considered a general purpose student for a semester; most of my work consisted of clearing the grounds where one of the buildings had recently burned on the campus. At the beginning of the second semester, my assignment was to take over the janitorial service in the chapel and feed the hogs twice daily. At this time I was eligible to eat three meals per day in the dining hall.

After two or three months on my new assignment, I discovered that there was a possibility that I could hustle enough food from the dining hall to feed two pigs of my own while feeding the school's hogs at the same time.

I talked the situation over with the president of the school, and he thought this was a good idea. So I purchased two pigs, gilts, so that I would have a rapid production. Before they were old enough to breed, I decided that the pigs would have to be sold as soon as they were ready to be weaned as I could not feed them beyond that stage. I knew that they should not be bred the first time they came in heat because I wanted them to grow to the fullest extent, and this would check their growth; therefore, I refused to breed them until they were around a year of age. Then I bred them and counted the days until (gestation) farrowing time, which is approximately three months. I was just like a father waiting for his first child to be born. They farrowed within a week or ten days apart; one had four pigs, and the other one had five. I was a bit disappointed as they didn't have more, but at the end of my second year, in Okolona Industrial School (OIS), I found myself failing in class work. They seemed to have liked my work, but it seemed that the harder I worked the more was assigned to me. I always like my jobs or maybe I should say, my work, because I've had many jobs I did not like, but I was taught to do the very best I could regardless to how I felt about the job.

> *If I should fail, when I have done my best,*
> *And striven well to meet each given test,*
> *I will not bow my head, but lift it up instead.*
> *(Author Unknown)*

For example, during real cold nights, I could hardly sleep because I fired the furnace, in addition to janitorial work there, and I always made a fire at least an hour earlier than normal on extremely cold days because I felt that this was a part of my training. I fed the hogs daily, on schedule, but they still felt that I had enough time in between these chores to go out and clean mortar off bricks and stack them as I did before my new assignment. Yet there were those who worked as they pleased and received as much recognition as I. I just barely made it through with my subject matter in my second year; occasionally I picked up a book to study and fell asleep. Sometimes I'd go to bed to sleep a while and get up early the next morning to study, but couldn't go to sleep because I knew I was failing. Luckily, I made it through my second year; but was determined not to repeat what I had done the year before.

In the meantime, I proceeded to go back to Southeast Missouri and try to go to Lincoln University, in Jefferson City, Missouri. Aunt Sid, who helped us out of Mississippi, did her utmost to help me to get to Lincoln, but all efforts failed. I fell in love with Okolona Industrial School and regretted the idea of having to leave; this was my first experience, one that I shall cherish the rest of my life. My English teacher, who was also Dean of the school, told me on one occasion that he'd like to see me become a member of that faith; had I stayed there, no doubt I would have joined the church. After having completed the tenth grade, I still made an effort to stay. My industrial arts teacher, who lived off the campus, had a small farm and wanted me to stay and work for him. I agreed to stay and moved in with him and wife and worked on the farm. During the middle of June, I could see that this arrangement did not meet with my approval. Therefore, I decided to sell my hogs and return to Missouri. I sold both sows and nine pigs for thirty-two dollars and fifty cents and hitchhiked back to Southeast Missouri.

During my two years at Okolona, I learned through correspondence about the farm where they specialized in raising pure bred, Hampshire hogs in Horn Lake, Mississippi, just across the state line, not too far from Memphis, Tennessee. At that time, they were supposed to have been the best hog for bacon, according to the meat packing company of Chicago. I discussed (with a few farmers) the possibility of purchasing this breed hog in southeast Missouri as it is one of the leading states in producing livestock and grain. Everyone seemed to have thought this was a good idea, with reservations as to whether this breed would be a good seller in that area, because they went in for such breeds as Polan China, Chester White and other mixed breeds. Pure bred livestock was not too popular in that area. I even talked the situation over with the county agent, Mr. Moore, who suggested that I follow through with my plans. In case southeast Missouri farmers didn't buy them, I could always sell them directly to the meat packers. This was all I needed. I took the thirty-two dollars and fifty cents and hitchhiked to the Gayoso Farm, in Horn Lake, Mississippi.

This was one of the most exciting moments of my life when I arrived at the farm which consisted of hundreds of acres and grew nothing except Hampshire hogs. All hogs sold on that farm were registered, and the color markings were very rigid; they had to be black with a white (solid) marking around the midsection. Occasionally a few were born that did not meet with this pattern; they could be purchased, but not registered. I decided to purchase two registered pigs for breeding purposes, and they cost fifteen dollars each. After the deal was closed, I told the landlord my situation and he made arrangements for me to stay overnight with one of the tenants on the farm, without charges; they were very nice people. In addition to overnight lodging, I was given an old fashioned, down home country dinner, which brought back many memories. I could hardly eat or sleep for thinking about the pigs which I had purchased, and it seemed that the next day would never dawn. After breakfast the next morning, I expressed my appreciation for their hospitality, bid them adieu, and hit the Highway #60 back to Missouri. My next job was to prepare a pen, in the backyard, in Caruthersville, Missouri where we lived. At that time, there was no law against such practice in the city limits.

The above transactions took place while we lived at Concord, Missouri. The first pig pen was (as described) built at Concord instead of Caruthersville. I then proceeded to attend high school at Caruthersville the last two years. Dad made plans for Niculia (Nickie) and me to stay with Mrs. Gilmore and two daughters for whatever he could afford, which was not very much. We stayed with the Gilmores only when school was in session, after which we returned to Concord to work on the farm and attend to the pigs which I purchased from the Gayoso Farm. The pigs were delivered to me during mid-winter, and the female took sick and died. And this was, to me, like losing a member of the family; I hardly knew just which way to turn. As to the veterinarian who saw these pigs upon arrival to Concord, he decided that changing climates during mid-winter caused the gilt to contract pneumonia, and this was the cause of her death. Through correspondence between him and the Gayoso Farm authorities, they gave me another gilt without charge along with new registration papers. I did all but sleep with these hogs in order to see that they received the best of care. Dad took care of them while I was in school.

While in high school my last year, a minister who owned a farm and lived in an adjacent county became interested in me and my affairs. He too had hogs, and gave me a Polan China pig which weighed approximately fifty pounds. And Mrs. Gilmore permitted me to keep it in her backyard until I graduated. I thought the best way to show appreciation for her kindness towards us was to give her this pig which at that time weighed approximately one hundred pounds. And she was as happy or happier than the money would have made her had the pig been brought to market. She informed me later that when she had it killed the following fall, it weighed more than two hundred and fifty pounds. She could not have been happier than I because we even shared food from her table with us. Her only source of income was from working for a private family along with what her two daughters were able to make doing part-time work after school and on weekends.

Mrs. Gilmore and daughters were very nice to us. In fact, I tried to convince the younger daughter that I wanted to be closer to her if she'd get closer to me. This was not the first time that I "fell in love with a gal who was in love with my pal.". The girls always seemed to like me but could not understand why I was five or six years behind in high school. Nickie and I finished high school together, and she is five years younger than me. I was twenty five years old when I finished high school, but I was determined not to let this come between me and an education.

The rougher the journey, the sweeter the success at
the end of the road. It's not where one comes from,
but where one plans to go that counts.

CROSSING THE BRIDGE

Chapter 2

I have fought many a battle and lost.
But I have won enough battles to forever believe
In the struggle, and to keep on fighting.

I have trusted many friends who failed me.
But I have known enough true friends to forever
Believe in Humanity and keep on trusting.

I have had many dreams that never came true.
But I have had enough dreams come true
To forever believe in the dream
And to keep on dreaming.

(Author Unknown)

Chapter 2

CROSSING THE BRIDGE

❖

Work

Throughout my high school career, I realized that my chances to go to college would be a struggle. Therefore, I decided to work as hard to obtain a job in the outside world as to try to get a job on any college campus in order to work my way through school. Back in those days, high school graduates could teach in elementary school. I made several applications to various schools in that area, and, of course, some paid better than others. Naturally, I preferred the better paying job, but I decided to take the first offer. While waiting, watching, and listening, I decided to go to summer school which served a multiple purpose. In the first place, it gave me a bit of exposure to those teachers who also attended summer school as well as superintendents and boards of education in that area. At last a favorable response came through for an interview to a district about six miles from Caruthersville, Missouri. Within a few days after the interview, I received a notice that I was being considered for the job, and the board of education wanted to hear from me immediately. I really didn't want the job because it only paid thirty dollars a month, but I could not afford to turn it down. I then proceeded to talk the situation over with those who had been teaching for a number of years. I was introduced to a Mrs. Augustus Hickman, who lived within walking distance from the school, but taught in another district too far away from home to commute. She therefore came home on weekends. She told me about her home situation, and that she and her husband owned a small farm, but rented to someone else. She further told me that her husband was a good man and not hard to get along with, but he was an alcoholic. I felt that I could put up with him, and that I could stay in their home (rent free). I reluctantly accepted the offer, but it was the best chance I had ever had, and I was not going there to stay. She talked it over with her husband prior to the time I met him, and the two agreed that I could stay. At a later date, the three of us met and agreed on the terms. I also told them that my stay would be only for a short time as I looked forward to going to college as soon as possible. I also told them that I had two pure-bred Hampshire pigs I'd like to bring with me if they had no objection. They kindly consented for me to bring the pigs and gave consent for me to fence a portion of their land on which to keep the hogs. They even furnished the wire and posts for the job. The name of the school was "Needmore," and at this time I began to put things together. Here I am pondering over the question as to whether I should accept the job for thirty dollars per month, or reject it, in hopes that something better would come my way. I finally decided that this deal was not too bad with a decent place to stay, without charges, for me and my hogs; and it was up to me as to what the cost for food would be. During mid-summer, I went to Needmore and fenced in the allotted plot for the hogs and made arrangements for a neighbor who had a truck to deliver the hogs on a specified date. I waited for the delivery until late in the afternoon. Afterwards, I became concerned as to what had happened to cause the delay. After having explained the situation to a local citizen who had a car, we decided to proceed to check the road between Needmore and Caruthersville to see just what caused the delay. We drove approximately two miles down the road (where three or four men were standing around the truck that was supposed to have made the delivery) to find that the gilt, female, had jumped over the side board of the truck to the ground and broke one of her hind legs, in fact, her hip. Therefore, she was no longer eligible to be used as a brood sow, but as any other hog on the market for meat purpose by the pound. So from then on, it was a matter as to just which way to go with the boar, or male. I wanted to replace the gilt, but couldn't afford another one at that time. I then decided to use the male for breeding purposes.

About a month after the tragedy in which my hog was involved, someone suggested that the person who made the delivery should have compensated for the damage as he was at fault. It was he who put the hogs on the truck and assumed that the sideboards were too tall for them to climb over. I immediately took the case to a lawyer on my next visit home to find that I had no case since I paid the man, and payment indicated that I was satisfied with his service.

I enjoyed my stay at Needmore. I thought I had learned how to live economically prior to this time, but I hadn't. During my stay at Needmore, my food cost anywhere from thirty-five to fifty cents a week. Not only did I teach school from first grade through eighth, but also I was always at school early enough to prepare my breakfast before the students arrived. There was a general store approximately five hundred feet below the school where I did my grocery shopping. I paid five cents for a loaf of bread, fifteen cents for a jar of jelly, and fifteen or twenty cents for a jar of peanut butter. I had a jelly sandwich for breakfast, peanut butter for lunch, and a combination of the two for dinner. For dessert I sometimes strained a point, and bought a three cent Baby Ruth. I kept my food in a locker in school.

Schools in southeast Missouri operated on what was called "a split season," that is, they opened during mid-summer which allowed time for a break when cotton opened around the first of September, in order to get the cotton picked, and so students would not lose time out of school during the season. And when we closed for this occasion, I joined the students with my cotton sack and picked cotton too. I too looked forward to cotton picking season; in fact, I learned to pick two hundred pounds per day. During that time I really made more money in the cotton patch than in the classroom as a teacher ($30.00 per month). The schools closed for approximately four weeks in order to pick the cotton. Later on, after cotton picking season was over, we had to close schools in our area again for a short period of time due to a flood which came as a result of an unusually rainy season.

In fact, the 1937 flood caused more than a few schools to close in that area, and this enabled me to join those who worked on the levy for a while and help place sand bags in order to control the water floor. I handled many sandbags during this time. I couldn't go home on weekends as often as I'd like for lack of transportation as well as money. And when I went home, I was forced to return to school on Sunday's when most youngsters were socializing. I had to hitchhike, and by all means be at school on time.

Frequently, when things didn't go my way, not too long afterward I could see a bit of sunshine just above the clouds. Not too long after the episode with my hog, I went home one weekend and visited a friend (fortune-teller) who lived across the street from us. He told me that he saw something in my future which looked very favorable; he further said that I would be leaving Caruthersville soon, and it appeared that I would be leaving the state of Missouri. Approximately two weeks later when I returned from school, one weekend I ran across my biology teacher. During our conversation which pertained to my future, he gave me a pat on the back for my continued effort to further my education. He mentioned Kentucky State College (now Kentucky State University) and asked if I would be interested in attending the college in case he got a job for me. I told him I would be very happy to go to Kentucky immediately, and that I felt that the board of education where I taught would understand my situation. I would recommend my sister, Niculia, to finish my unexpired term which was two months. He wrote a letter recommending me to his former classmate, Mr. J. D. Stewart, who worked in the Business Office at Kentucky State and was Assistant Football Coach at the College. Mr. Stewart turned the letter over to Mr. M. T. (Plank) Woods who was head of the Department of Agriculture. Mr. Woods in turn wrote me a nice letter in which he gave a brief description of the only job available on the farm. He also included an application for me to fill out, if interested. I never before had been so happy as when this letter arrived. The job consisted of regular farm work which I had done throughout my life. After having shared the information with the family, I took off to the fortune teller's house across the street and shared the same with him. He in turn reminded me of what he had told me a few days prior to this time. I never did pay any attention to those who were suppose to tell one far in advance what the future had in store for him, even though Rev. Carter made a living in this occupation. There were those who came to his house twenty-four hours daily, and paid him to tell them what the future had in store for them. From then on I became "a believer."

Reverend Carter had a church, thirty some miles away in Elythville, Arkansas, which I never paid any attention to until this time. I asked if I might visit his church sometime, and he gave his consent. And he preached on foretelling the future. I now recall the time when he told me that I was going to leave the state of Missouri was during one of his special meetings at his house. He invited the public to attend ever so often. I attended one of his sessions, out of curiosity, at which time he lectured on foretelling the future. At the end of his lecture, he suggested that everyone who wished to know something about his future should kneel in a semicircle and bow his head with closed eyes. He went from one to another placing his hands on each head and gave a three minute forecast on what

53

the future had in store for him. This was his way of advertising his business. This is my reason for having gone to him to share the information which I received from Kentucky. He encouraged me to accept the offer without reservation. I reluctantly went home and shared the encouraging opinion with my parents who were of the same opinion I had (prior to this time) regarding fortune tellers. I could see Dad turning "thumbs down" on the Reverend's opinion for two reasons: first, he had no confidence in fortune tellers, and secondly he would no longer be able to depend on me to help support the family. But I could also see the possibility of my future being worse than Dad's in the not too distant future if I failed to do something immediately. I was twenty-five years of age with only a high school diploma. I had been engaged to get married on two different occasions, but could see myself being worse off than my parents if I lived long enough. It seemed that those who were less qualified to support a family had more children than anybody.

> I have fought many a battle and lost,
> but I have won enough battles to forever
> believe in the struggle, and to keep on fighting.
> I have trusted many friends who failed me,
> but I have had enough true friends,
> to forever believe in humanity and to keep on trusting.
> I have had many dreams that never came true,
> but I have had enough dreams come true
> to forever believe in the dream,
> and to keep on dreaming.
>
> *(Author Unknown)*

I have never regretted not having followed through with matrimony with the two women whom I dearly loved. The first one did not go to college, but I was told by a friend, while visiting in Mississippi in 1987, that she got married to a man in Michigan who is now decreased. However, he left her an independent lady able to live a decent life. The second one was fortunate in marrying a farmer who owned a decent farm in southeast Missouri and made an independent living. They reared and educated a son who now holds a masters degree. Both parents have deceased, but they left the son able to live a decent life if he follows through on what he was taught, both at home and in school.

I finally decided to fill out the application and sent it to Mr. Woods at Kentucky State College for fear Mr. Woods would get the idea that I had reservations about the job since it only paid seven dollars and fifty cents cash per month. I decided to precede the application with a telegram which read as follows: "Terms OK. Application will follow." I also completed the application the same day and mailed it. In the meantime my parents and I had a heart-to-heart discussion regarding my final decision to go to Kentucky State College. Mother had told me that Dad felt I was withholding my money from them. I didn't mention this while we all were together, but later on during that same day, Dad and I furthered the discussion out in the backyard. I told him I had only sixty dollars and feared I would need it, and maybe more, during the move to Kentucky. He reluctantly agreed. While waiting to receive notice from Kentucky State confirming my being accepted at the college, I also discussed the plan with my board of education and recommended my sister, Niculia, to finish the year, which was only two months.

College

At the end of my seventh month at Needmore, I received a letter which stated that I had been accepted at Kentucky State College in Frankfort, Kentucky. It said that they would be expecting me the first of April, 1937. My sister, Niculia, finished the school term. As hard as I had worked over the past ten years for this opportunity, it was one of the most difficult tasks for me to say goodbye to my family whom I dearly loved. What did Shakespeare say about this type of situation? "Not that I love Rome less, but I love me best." I didn't love my family less, but I had love for me and my future family best. I decided to come to Frankfort by bus as my job seemed more secure than any other over a period of ten years.

55

I left Caruthersville, Missouri a day early in order to spend a night in Paducah with Dad's oldest brother and his family whom I had not seen for years. They were happily surprised at my arrival as they were not notified that I had planned to be their overnight guest. The Simmons family is noted for kissing the women, but this was my first experience to kiss a man -- especially one with a mouthful of fever-blisters. Uncle Eugene's wife prepared a delicious dinner, and we ate and talked, and stayed up about two thirds of the night. The next morning, Aunt Pet, as we called her, prepared breakfast, and I was off to the bus station in order to catch the first bus that morning to Frankfort. Again, I had the experience of kissing a mouth that was filled with fever-blisters. I arrived in Frankfort in the early afternoon and got off the bus at the Training Home, or Feebleminded Institute, as it was commonly called, thinking this was Kentucky State College, to find that I was less than a block from the college.

I took off in the rain to the college. Those who saw me running in the rain perhaps thought I was protecting myself from the rain, but instead it was the cardboard suit case I was protecting. I was directed to Mr. Wood's office, and after a briefing as to what the farm program was all about, he took me to the farm across Highway #60, about three- fourths of a mile from the college, where I met twelve other students who had been assigned to the farm duties. We lived in the old slave house, which looked like Heaven to me. The farm consisted of two hundred and sixty acres of land. Being an agricultural training institution was a distinct advantage because the farm was utilized not only for teaching but also to feed the student body and faculty.

Located high on a hill in a particularly beautiful part of this lush land, stood the remains of the one-time elegant mansion which later became the men's dormitory. When the land was purchased for the college, the house was part of the deal. Facing sunshine, it overlooked a beautifully-contoured valley, and just below it, nestled close to the hill, was the old spring house that was the first waterworks for the college. The old mansion was in pretty good condition, but the interior had been neglected for so many years that it seemed to have been almost beyond recall. The basement of this building is what posed the irony of the situation, for located underneath this once-grand home were extensive slave quarters. Dank and dark, they sent a shiver up the spine and made you want to

56

dash back outside to the bright day.   Although this mansion may have represented slavery to many blacks over a hundred years ago, it was Emancipation to me as I arrived here from Caruthersville, Missouri, back in 1937.   I realized at an early age that the real key to the freedom of blacks and other races lies in education.   I pledged to spend a life-time proving this philosophy.

Good things come to him who waiteth providing he worketh like hell while he waiteth.

In addition to the farmhouse, there was the dairy barn where the cows and mules were kept, and a silo which we filled during the summer for cow feed during the winter. The second deck of the barn was used to store corn and hay for the five mules and one horse during winter. There were also houses for shelter for both hogs and chickens as well as the farm shop where we practiced maintaining our own farming equipment. There were also pastures for all livestock. The dining department received the greater portion of its fruits and vegetables from the farm as well as beef and pork. The leghorn poultry was grown for its egg-producing quality. Each student was assigned certain responsibilities, but we all pitched in and milked the cows by hand twice daily in order to see that the milk got to the dining hall on time. We did our own slaughtering, both beef and pork, during early fall. The wagon, drawn by two mules, was used not only to deliver milk and eggs to the dining hall, but also food from the dining hall three times daily for those who worked on the farm. We were called "farm boys," but they always saw to it that we got our portion of food at mealtime; in fact, many times we had leftovers which we munched on during the day between meals.

The majority of those who lived on the farm were Kentuckians and went home frequently, but I couldn't afford to visit home because of the lack of money. Therefore, I always looked forward to substituting for those who had campus jobs in order to make extra money. I was always glad when Jean Davidson took a leave from the campus because he allowed me to work as a bellhop at the Southern Hotel while he was absent. I recall one occasion when Matthew Brooks, who also lived on the farm, told me that he always took his leave during tobacco harvest time and how well one was paid for working in tobacco. And I looked

57

forward to doing likewise the next season. But I was somewhat skeptical, having come from the cotton farms of Mississippi and Southeast Missouri, and had never seen tobacco before, but I had a feeling that anybody who had worked on a Mississippi cotton plantation should be able to harvest tobacco.

Matthew had me well schooled by the next season, and I took a two-week leave with him to Little Rock, just out of Paris, Kentucky in Bourbon county (his hometown), and we agreed not to tell the farm owner that I had no experience in working in tobacco because of fear that he would not pay me the same wage that he paid others. I felt that with the pre-schooling prior to that time I could defend myself. So we took off to Little Rock on Friday evening for two weeks, and on the following Monday we reported to a Mr. Clark Thomas for work. He started us out plucking suckers from the stalk. For a day or two, I'd find it convenient to choose the row next to Matthew so he could evaluate my work in terms of speed and accuracy. It thrilled me when he said that I was doing as well as anybody else, but he had no idea how soft my fingers were as a result of not knowing that there was an art in the job, and until one learned it, it was just one of those things. I was reminded of many times my fingers had to be taped in the cotton patch as a result of burr snags which occurred while trying to pick the lent at a rapid pace. When we completed the job with Mr. Thomas, and he had paid me, I told him that I never worked in tobacco before. He complimented me and said I did as well as anybody. From there I went to the second farmer with confidence and sore fingers, but did the job satisfactorily. When we returned to the farm after two weeks, I stopped in Lexington and bought my first bathrobe, black trimmed in red, for seven dollars and fifty cents. I had more cash than ever before during my first two years in Kentucky, except money made from selling clothes to students and a few townspeople during the second semester of my first year.

I brought suit samples to Frankfort which I purchased when we lived in Jonestown, Mississippi from the Great Western Tayloring Company of Chicago, Illinois. I showed them to the fellows on the farm and told them I'd measure them for clothes wholesale if they'd quote the retail price to others in order to get started in the tailoring business on campus. This we did, and my business was a huge success. One of our agriculture teachers called me one night to inform me that the band was planning to buy suits, twelve, the next day down to Shelbyville,

Kentucky. I called the band director immediately and gave him the same proposition I was giving the boys on the farm. It commensurated with the Shelbyville company in price, but was superior in quality. I gave them four dollars off my commission and charged them only a dollar per suit. They accepted the offer, and we were in business.

Immediately after having measured the Kentucky State College band for suits, I went to the post office to mail a money order. This was the time when one had to use ink blotters and the old fashioned ink pen found conveniently in the lobby of post offices. I completed my application for a money order and reached for an ink blotter to find that the one I got had my name on it as sales representative for the Great Western Tailoring Company, Chicago, Illinois. Then it came to me that the company had written to me a few days before this time. They wanted to know more about Kentucky State College, and I responded immediately upon having received the request or questionnaire.

When the company completed the order and the fellows got their clothes, the company gave me a suit and extra pair pants as a bonus. I had a classmate from Harrodsburg, Kentucky by the name of Lacona Williams, who was an art major, to draw a "Zuit Suit." It had an extra long coat, pants with pleats, extra large through the hips and small bottom with a narrow cuff. This was mounted on a cardboard approximately five feet tall with a statement attached which read as follows:

Suits for the band were made
by the
Great Western Tailoring Company
of
Chicago, Illinois
George W. Simmons, Jr., Salesman.

From that day hence, I spent a great part of my time selling clothes on the campus, and I had quite a number of customers in the downtown area of Frankfort. I also had quite a few women customers for slacks and two and three piece suits. I was very happy when a couple, husband and wife, ordered suits (black) from the same material, or pattern. I had only two customers whose garments had to be returned to the Company for alterations. The first one was one of my co-workers on the farm, whose hickory-striped trousers were too large in the hips. This was when the Zuit Suits came out, and I had to learn how to correlate the hips to coincide with the knees and bottom, at the shoe top. The other one was a minister whose coat had to be altered through the shoulders. The company gave me a bonus: a pair of pants for three suit orders within a month's time, and a suit for five suits within that time. From then on I never had to worry about clothes; in fact, I had a friend on the farm who often wore my clothes on different occasions. He was the friend who took me to the tobacco patch for the first time. However, the money I made during my second year, in 1938, got me in trouble with my classwork.

Many times my mind went back to Jonestown, Mississippi where Mother had to borrow money from one of her women's auxiliaries to get the suit from the post office, on Sunday morning, after all other attempts had failed. After having worn the suit a few times before it needed cleaning, someone in the family placed a kerosene lamp, lighted, on a table under my suit which was hanging on the wall. It burned the coat in front at the bottom where it came together when buttoned, and Mother (being a seamstress) was able to get enough material to patch it from inside of the coat without it being noticeable. Coat hangers were unknown in those days. We made our own by cutting a twig from a bush about the length of a clothes hanger and attaching a cord string in the center to hang by. It left approximately one inch in the center with a loop or beau in order to hang the garment on a nail. This method applied to coats only; pants were attached to the coat, by the cuffs with safety pins. We did our own cleaning with a gasoline solution which was mixed with water, and we pressed the garments.

To press men's clothes, there was a special iron, ranging in weight from fifteen pounds to twenty-two pounds so that special emphasis could be placed on the creases with the aide of dampness, having sprinkled the garment with water and placed a towel on the garment while pressing. This is where the steam came about. My Uncle Walter Whitehead taught many youngsters in the community how to press their own clothes. He only charged fifty-cents to clean and press a suit. Creases not only applied to pants, but coats as well. Coats were out of style if they didn't have a crease in the sleeves as well as the back. Caps were even creased.

I was not allowed to wear long pants until my mid-teens, and perhaps it would have been later, had it not been for a cousin who came to visit from Toledo, Ohio. He had several suits, some of which were too small for him and were just right for me. When my parents gave their permission for me to wear long pants, I felt like a man. Prior to this time I, like most others, wore knee pants with long underwear which extended down in our stockings just above the shoe top. Many times when we were out of sight from our parents, we pulled the underwear out of our stockings and anchored them above the knee until time to go home or before our parents wherever they were. Hightop shoes, in most cases, were to be worn during winter and low quarters in summer.

When I came to Kentucky State College, I wore long draws, as the boys often referred to them as "long funky draws" (LFD's). I paid very little attention to this until I found that the girls on the main campus did the students' laundry to defray their expenses. Many had jobs both on the campus and downtown or otherwise could not be in school. I was somewhat upset over this situation for fear the girl which I was interested in would get the news. I tried leaving them off during the winter, but this was most miserable when the weather was cold. It was especially bad going to and fro from the farm to class and vice versa. At times my legs got so cold they had very little feeling, and on Tuesdays and Thursdays we took gym. When other members of the class entered the gymnasium, they went in dropping their pants and shirts while I had to go down stairs to the dressing room and pull off my long draws in order to put on my gym suit. When the class was over, they put on their pants and shirts while I had to go down stairs to the dressing room and pull off my long draws in order to put on my gym suit. When the class was over, they put their pants and shirts on as they went out, and I had to go back to the dressing room and change for the next class. We had only ten minutes between classes; therefore, it rushed me to make the next class on time. When I got there, I was so warm I was forced to farm while others were comfortable. One of the farm boys, whom I thought much of, told me one day that I'd better either wear my draws every day or pull them off for good, or I might come up with pneumonia. This worried me to no end, but I finally decided to wear

61

them every day during winter and wash them on the farm myself. They became quite dingy, but I tried to keep them out of sight to others. I bought my first radio while on the farm. It was a Crosley, secondhand, and cost twelve dollars and fifty cents. Those who listened to it, in my absence violated the law because I *and I only* was to have given permission to turn it on.

During the second semester, someone told me about the National Youth Administration (NYA) and what benefits were available for those who qualified. I went by the business office immediately and got an application, took it to the farm, and filled it out the same day. I submitted it to that office the following day, and when the business manager, Reverend J.H. Ingraham, looked it over, I noticed he paused for a minute or two as though something was incomplete in my way of filling out the application. Finally he came with this statement, "Mr. Simmons, I'm sorry, but it looks as though you are too old to qualify for this program." When he got through talking to me about how much he admired me for may ambition and what I had gone through in order to get to Kentucky State College, and what the job meant to me if I did a good job on the farm for the rest of my college career, I felt like a new person. But the question came to me, "Just what was I to tell the fellows on the farm when they found that I didn't qualify for the NYA?" There was one other among the farm boys who was older than me, but he was a junior when I arrived. I couldn't come up with anything except the truth because they would have found out just why I didn't qualify at a later day.

This was when I thanked God for William (Bill) Elster who was a year or two older than I, but he was in his third year. They called him "Abe" for Abraham Lincoln. I was still encouraged to have known him, as each of us had something in common. They called him "Abe Lincoln" because he felt that the truth was always best. Shakespeare wrote,

Truth lies on the lips of dying men, and falsehood, while I lived, was far from mine.

My co-workers on the farm and a few others who majored in agriculture called me "Reb" for Reverend because of my age and sincerity. Many times I wondered if those who knew very little about me thought I was going through the change at an early age, or whether I misrepresented my age or was older than I said I was. I was made Chaplain of my class during my first two years at Kentucky State. These names for Bill and me were not only used by the boys on the farm, but throughout the Department of Agriculture and by many other students. I was always known as the class Chaplin.

It often comes to my mind, in reminiscence, that I wished I could be like many of those whom I knew in college. That is, they made good grades and wore good clothes. As a result of their backgrounds, everybody knew them because of their parents, and this kind of situation caused some to get by in school because of their backgrounds. Some were able to get into the Greek letter organizations, etc., because of these kinds of situations. I found that some faculty members took special interest in those students coming from popular families or those who made "A's" and were popular in the Greek letter organizations and graduated on time with honors. But when I showed up here in 1937, just out of high school at age 25 and not knowing anybody, and no one knew me or any of my people, I had to make it on my own. If I had had a good scholastic record it would have helped me, maybe. However, I followed a few beyond college days to find that they found that it's good to make "A's" in school, but to mix a bit of common sense in between helps to make one a good citizen. The classroom teachers in some cases lead the poor student to believe if he couldn't make an "A," and didn't belong to "the great society," there was no place in the community for him. However, I've had many interviews and was told that on an average, the "C" student usually makes the best adjustment in the community. This is where I felt that some faculty members at K-State made a big mistake in placing too much emphasis on students whose parents were of the upper crust in the society and had a little money, maybe, at least that impression was given. But very little was known about the background of the average student whose parents were unheard of in the society.

It's your attitude AND NOT your aptitude that determines your latitude.

It was noted that most students from the Deep South with big families had to work on plantations where the landlord told them that they didn't need an education because he'd take care of them. The school systems were of the poorest

63

in the land, and those who strived to raised themselves above this standard of life were in small numbers and were looked down on by the majority. Regardless of how good the teachers were, they could do just so much in the one-room schools which were common in that area. Many times I tried to give up and join the gang, but Mother was always there when I needed her most. I can hear her ever so often saying,

"Son, don't give up even if you are fifty years old when you get out. You can live the rest of your life." Mind you, men didn't live much older than fifty back in those days, but I believed in her and refused to give up. If more teachers in colleges looked at students from a different view, where they are trying *to go* instead of where they came *from*, and made an extra effort in trying to help them, we would have a better world in which to live.

❖

Military

I was inducted into the military service April 16, 1942 at Camp Atterbury, Indiana, and was discharged from Camp Atterbury, Indiana, October 17, 1945. My experience in the military service was priceless. At the beginning of World War II, when the United States went into intensive training in an effort to prepare for that war, there were forty officers from Kentucky, Indiana and Ohio sent to Camp Shelby, Mississippi to train soldiers. Each of the above mentioned states was given a chance to select or recommend employees to take care of the officers' quarters. Six men were chosen from Kentucky; I was chosen to attend bar, as I had prior experience in that job. I liked the job for more than one reason. In the first place, I made more money. Secondly, we felt that this would prolong my stay out of the armed forces, if not exempt me. One army officer who was Commissioner of the Department of Economic Security for the State of Kentucky knew me as a bartender at one of the local bars and liked the way I made his favorite drink. He took me to Camp Shelby, Mississippi as a bartender for forty officers at the beginning of WWII. He told me that if we, he and I, survived during or after the war, he planned to return to Frankfort and resume his duties as Commissioner of the Department of Economic Security. He said if he could help me in any way to get in touch with him. Within three weeks after we were in Mississippi, my fiancee's mother passed away; when I received this news, I decided to return to Frankfort, not only for the funeral, but to get married. At first we had decided to wait until the war was over before getting married, but after this happened we decided to get married immediately after the funeral as both of her parents were deceased, and she had neither sister or brother. When I told this to the Colonel, he understood and expressed appreciation for my having told him the facts instead of giving him the impression that I'd be back. The commanding officer wanted me to return to camp after the funeral, but my friend had no other close family ties. We had decided to get married immediately after World War II, so we got married immediately after her mother's funeral. I informed the officers at camp that this was a strong possibility before I left, and they commended me for having told them this in advance instead of waiting until I got home. They wished me well, and the Colonel (who was a commissioner in state government) told me that if there was anything he could do for me after the war to let him know. Knowing that I was eligible to become drafted into the service, I resumed my old job as a bartender and got married in April 1941. A year later, I was drafted into the Army.

I spent nine months in basic training at Fort Leonard Wood, Missouri. At the conclusion of basic training, I was able to spend a weekend in St. Louis, Missouri with my wife who met me there. After that, a group of us was shipped to Fort Custer, Michigan by box cars, just as any other animals. Two days after having arrived to Ft. Custer, we received orders to start packing for overseas duty. I had tonsillitis since early childhood, but our parents were not able to have them removed. At that time I was glad, because I didn't think I would be shipped overseas under those circumstances. On the third day at Fort Custer, I reported on sick call to the infirmary, and the doctor hospitalized me immediately. I felt that I'd be left when the unit shipped out for overseas duty, and I could see myself being stationed in Michigan for a period. To me, anything would have been better than going overseas, especially at that time when the World War II was just beginning. Two days after surgery, I was sent back to the barracks to join the 94th Engineers to be shipped out for overseas duty two days later. I did everything possible to induce bleeding, thinking that would keep me from going with the unit. They had even packed my belongings and taken my bed down, and I had to sleep on the floor for two nights prior to our departure. The third day we boarded a train, instead of boxcars. There were several carloads, but this time it was a train for passengers, instead of boxcars.

No one seemed to have known just where we were going (military secret) for our protection. It was said at that time that "a slip of the lip, sinks ships." We finally arrived in Fort Dix, New Jersey. And we were to have been shipped out from there within a matter of hours. We stayed at Fort Dix, however, nine months waiting for orders to be shipped out to Europe for duty (ETO) European Theater of Operation. Fort Dix is located just out of Trenton, New Jersey and conveniently located from Philadelphia, New York and Washington, D.C. Many soldiers kept the railway and highways hot during our nine months there. I went

66

to New York only once while there; it was too fast and expensive for me. My wife visited with me once while there.

While at Fort Dix, I was told to report to the Company Headquarters, which came as a surprise. In fact, I had mixed emotions, because, in most cases when one received such orders in the military service, it was because he had either done something wrong or he had not done what was expected of him. It couldn't have been the way I kept my bed or uniform or my rifle, because I hadn't been issued a rifle. As I went, I tried to come up with just what this was all about, and finally when I arrived I was told that they had reduced the company clerk to private(Pvt) because of something he had done wrong, and that they were in need of a detachment clerk. They saw in my records that I could type; so they wanted to know if I wanted the job. I hardly knew just what to say because I'd never had a lesson, in the classroom, as such, but my roommate at Okolona Industrial Junior College, Okolona, Mississippi, periodically told me about his assignments. I spent a portion of my time doing what he had done in class while cleaning the business office, as I was the janitor of that particular classroom. He encouraged me to take the course, but this was impossible as it was not in my curriculum, and as my janitorial work kept me so busy it was too much to attempt and keep up in my class work. But they gave me the job, and I must have done a pretty good job because I was retrained as company clerk throughout my military career, nine months at Fort Dix and two years and eleven months in Europe. My biggest problem was to keep an accurate account of each soldier's service record. If this was not accurate, it caused the soldier to be redlined and therefore, not paid on time. I must have done a pretty good job. This was quite an honor because those who worked in the headquarters did not have to do guard duty or follow the strict rules of keeping their rifles for inspection around the clock, especially in the theater of operation where fighting was going on. I'm sure Peter Hodge would have been thrilled to know how much it meant to me then that he taught me the fundamentals of typing.

A man is like a tack, he goes no further than his head will let him.

This was a prestigious job for those who worked in the personnel office; you got to know more about the soldiers through their service records. For example, before going into the personnel office I'd been told that I was the only one in my outfit from downhome, Mississippi. When I became familiar with my job to the extent that I had time to go through each service record of those in my outfit, I found that there were only two fellows in my outfit who were not from downhome. And when I went to the barracks, I took them one by one, beginning with the first sergeant, who was from (originally) Rome, Georgia, instead of Detroit, Michigan; from then on I had no more trouble with the boys who claimed where they were enlisted from as home, instead of their native homes.

Knowledge means power.

We were a medical unit, attached to the 94th Engineers, and our duties were to take care of soldiers who needed medical care, such as first aid or hospitalization. The 94th Engineers were responsible for such duties as building roads and bridges behind the firing line. When I became detachment clerk, I was exempted from first aide duties except on an emergency basis.

The trip to and throughout Europe was one that I shall never forget, except for a few things that I'd love to forget. For example, the nine-day voyage from Fort Dix, New Jersey without escort to North Africa on the British Andise was unbelievable. I had a short furlough home just before we were shipped out to North Africa, Casa Blanca, which was kept a secret until we arrived. Information relative to what was happening to ships at sea was seldom available to the enlisted man, and naturally we always expected the worse. Many soldiers were sea sick throughout the nine days . We were told that suffering the most from sea sickness was due to not eating hardy, especially at meal time. I did not like the food in the first place, and not knowing just what might happen to the ship at any time, we looked for the worse. Therefore I was sea sick throughout the voyage. We landed in Casa Blanca, North Africa on the ninth day. Those who ate most were the least sick; not only did they eat hardy at mealtime, but several also ate between meals. We were in Casa Blanca six months repairing and building roads and bridges.

68

Many local citizens, Arabs, were hired by the engineers and did excellent jobs. Bickles were their means of transportation, and donkeys and a few camels were used for transportation. The majority had no means of transportation and therefore, walked to and from work. Their lunch, in most cases, consisted of brown bread (which was carried unwrapped), a bottle of wine (vino), and grasshoppers, which were either boiled or roasted like popcorn and eaten whole, similar to our way of eating popcorn, etc. We were not allowed to share food with them; it was not uncommon to see them picking discarded food from the garbage cans. And mind you, much of this kind of food was not edible. Coffee and other liquids were discarded in the same can as solids. A friend from Akron, Ohio and I fell in love with two little Arabian girls. In fact, we wanted to adopt them, but it was impossible at that particular time because of the war situation. My wife and I were childless, and my friend was not even married at that time. After our job was finished in Casa Blanca, we went to Iran for a brief stay before going to Southern France, Marseilles, a fortified seaport on the west coast of Sicily. A light colored wine was made in Marseilles, similar to Kentucky as a bourbon state. Instead of using a press to separate the juice from the berry, they placed it in several sacks, and several employees were used to tramp over the sacks in order to separate the juice from the berry.

The Arabians were using cocaine (Kief) during World War II ; it was not uncommon to travel on the highways and see citizens of that country lying on the wayside smoking kief or cocaine, sometimes passed out. But it seemed that they lived a normal life; one could count those who were obese, or excessively fat, on one hand, and evidentally the bread and wine contained the necessary vitamins for survival, along with the grasshoppers. I never heard of a doctor or hospital throughout our stay in North Africa; at times I wondered if some of those who sustained injuries did so in order to receive first aide from our first aide stations. They displayed band aids as though they were some form of decoration. The majority of the citizens in that area wore robes, made in the form of a sack with three holes in it for the head and arms. Many soldiers were disciplined or subjected to punishment for having sold mattress covers, for a singular bed, for twenty dollars in North Africa. They considered this as a suit of clothes. I sold quite a few candy bars for two or three dollars each; there was also a great demand for cigarettes and soap, both toilet and laundry. Cognac was a popular drink throughout Europe similar to our bourbon. The Arabians had many wives who did most of the work on the farm; it was common to see the husband riding his donkey to and from work while the wives walked and carried whatever they produced on the farm, or the tools which they worked with, or both on their heads.

I wouldn't take anything for my military experience; neither would I like to go back through it again. I would like to return to Europe in peace time in order to see the many changes that have taken place over the years. Marseilles, France, a seaport city, was just like going to Florida. I went to Paris only once, similar to going to New York. A coke in New York cost twenty-five cents during World War II; I went there only once. I mailed most of my money home to my wife, who did a beautiful job by saving it. On one occasion, while in France, I received a letter from her which described a two piece, black, suit which she liked and wanted to know if I thought sixty dollars was too much to pay for it. And mind you, it took from thirty to sixty days, or more for mail coming from the United States to reach Europe during that time. Immediately I gave approval, hoping that it would still be in style by the time she received my reply. This made me very happy to feel that she not only respected me, but also the law of economy. It was not uncommon to hear stories from other servicemen regarding the way their loved ones were spending their money as fast as it was received, or before. One of my personal friends, whose name also was George, told me that he had received a letter from his wife which contained every penny he had sent her. The reason was, that she had had a baby by another man and felt that she could not keep his money under said conditions. She continued to keep in touch, and he told me that he felt that they would remain as husband and wife, if she would agree. But he also had reservations as to what would become of the child. Of course, we found this story worked both ways between soldiers and their mates; there were those who deserted their mates for other women, even before we left the states, as well as those who did likewise for women overseas. Since I sent most of my money home, I had to borrow from friends occasionally. But when I was discharged, I found that my wife had saved every penny that I had sent home. I was happy to know this, but I also had mixed emotions because I wanted her to feel free to spend as she saw fit. She said she wanted a home and had saved enough for a down payment. And this was the beginning of our first home.

Even though our travel in Europe came as a result of World War II, it was quite educational. We went from North Africa to France and then to Italy and finally into Germany where we were making plans to go to Japan when the war ended. Instead of continuing our preparation to go to Japan, immediately we began to prepare to return to the good old USA. At this point, we were given an eight-day leave, wherever we chose, so long as we could return to the unit within eight days. Many chose to return to some of the places we had been, but many wanted to go to some place where we had never been. I chose Switzerland, which I never regretted. Switzerland is the most beautiful country I've ever seen; besides cleanliness, flowers were displayed not only in and around the dwellings, but at public buildings as well. Germany ranked second. Even though it was engaged in war, clean women worked on the farm dressed as though they were going to a social affair. Even though much of their country was uprooted by war, there were no flies to be seen. Everything they did was well done. We always looked forward to eating the food which German prisoners of war prepared because they did it well, like home cooking. We bragged about our modern highways, interstates, or cleverness, but they had them during World War II (called the *Autobahn*). Italy reminds me much of our own society when it comes to locations. The Sicilians (Sicily), which is a part of Italy, did not associate with the Italians in southern Italy, and the Napoleons in Naples did not recognize the Sicilians. Neither were they claimed by Italians in central or northern Italy, similar to our American society. We had a fellow in our outfit from New Orleans who only finished the sixth grade but spoke foreign languages better than those from America who had degrees in foreign languages and taught here in our country. I met Pope Pius XII while in Rome, and had a rosary blessed by him for my late wife's cousin who is Catholic. Saint Die, a cathedral town on the Meruthe River in northeast France was quite interesting; this is where our Statue of Liberty originated. When we returned to our unit after an eight-day furlough, we were rerouted to the good old USA, instead of Japan.

To return home was the best homecoming I've ever known. The journey was much smoother, and we had no fear except for mines that were in our pathway that maybe hadn't been cleared away. The experience we had from the time we left for Europe up to that time was a great help. We returned to America by way of Brussels, Belgium, and then to New York, where the Statue of Liberty looked better, for various reasons, than it did on our way to Europe, and the visit to Saint Die. Even the return to Camp Atterbury, Indiana looked better than before, when I was inducted into the military service on April 16, 1942.

But I found that things had not changed very much, if any, between the time I was inducted and October 17, 1945 when I was discharged. For example, I had a friend from Ashland, Kentucky (who happened to have been White) whom I admired very much. We thought alike, especially when it came to our American society compared to that which we'd experienced in Europe. We spent many days together in Europe, but didn't realize our last night was when we landed in New York. We road the bus together from New York to camp Atterbury, Indiana, and there we were directed to segregated barracks. After having received our discharge papers, we took the bus to Louisville, Kentucky the next day. In Louisville we changed buses to Frankfort. Being among the first to board the bus, we thought we could choose our own seats; therefore, we chose the seat behind the driver and thought nothing about it. When the driver entered the bus, he paused for a minute and finally turned to me and said, "You have to take a seat in the back." I went to the back, with my "good old" American uniform on with five battle stars and a Good Conduct Medal displayed on my uniform. I was disappointed to learn that change had not come to our "good old" America. We stopped at the halfway house between Shelbyville and Frankfort on Highway 60 so that those who chose to get food could do so. Bailey refused to get off the bus so that we could discuss our racial problem here at home. We both pledged that we would change our uniform or get into our civilian clothes, but must roll up our sleeves and continue the battle here at home for justice for all as well as freedom. When I said goodbye to Bailey here in Frankfort as he proceeded to Ashland, we promised to keep in touch. We did for a number of years, but somehow we lost touch with each other over the years.

When I met my wife around three o'clock that morning, October 17, 1945, I had mixed emotions, just to think of all that had been said and done during World

War II towards freedom for all and all the lives that had been lost. The struggle was in vain.

The laws of changeless justice bind, oppressors with oppressed, and close as sin
and suffering join, we march to fate abreast.
(Author Unknown)

It was difficult for me to get around to expressing my feelings to my wife because she did not understand; in fact, it was almost impossible to explain the situation to one who had never been involved in world conflict as we had been. We finally got around to discuss the situation, but each agreed that this is our homeland, and the best we could do is to "cast down our bucket where we are" and be good citizens. Things have gradually changed over the years, but still we have quite a distance in go in order to enjoy equality. There is much to be done on both sides of the railroad track in order to improve our society.

I met quite a number of local fellows who were discharged before me who said that we World War II vets were eligible for twenty dollars per month for fifty-two weeks after discharge. Many were already signed up for a year. At first thought, I thought this was nice, thinking that this was because there were no jobs available, but before I signed I found that there were jobs available. Even though they were not what I preferred, I took a job with the state as a janitor hoping that something better would come my way in the not too distant future. The pay was not much better than the 52-20, but I always liked to earn my living. With only two years of college, there was not much one could get in the way of a half-way decent job. I worked at several jobs during this time, trying to adjust after having failed in college during my second semester. I worked at the corner drug store as a delivery boy, an attendant at the service station washing cars and fixing flats, a janitor, a bartender, janitor at the theater, a bell-hop at one of the local hotels, a messenger at the local bank, and a truck driver at a furniture store; none of these sufficed. I had to give up the furniture store because the handling of the heavy furniture was too much. The system they used involved taking furniture from one floor to another where the elevator only went to the second floor, and much furniture was to be taken to and from the third and fourth floor. I failed to mention the ladies ready-to-wear store, where women came in and selected a number of dresses and had them delivered to their homes on approval. After which, if they didn't keep any, the store was given a call to have those returned to the store. The owner felt that I would make a good salesman and wanted me to take a course in salesmanship on the GI Bill which was quite a challenge. Other responsibilities were attached, however, such as keeping the building clean and firing the furnace during the winter. Maybe I should mention another job which was of a very short duration. During this time in the mid-40's, the city of Frankfort decided to make East Main wider, four lanes instead of the original two lanes from the "new bridge," as it was known at that time, to a point beyond K-State. I decided to apply for a job, was hired, and assigned to the jack hammer. The pay was super, a bit beyond minimum wage, but I couldn't handle that jackhammer. This was my first, and last, experience with that tool. I even fought, in my sleep, for three nights, or maybe I should say it fought me three nights. I couldn't sleep for running that jack hammer in my sleep. The boss was a bit disappointed when I reported on the fourth day, not to work, but to inform him that I could no longer operate the jack hammer. So, it was after I'd failed in college and gone out into the cold cruel world and found what I had to face the rest of my life without an education that I made the decision to return to the classroom.

❖

Graduation from College

At this time I began to think seriously about my future. After having
flunked out in college and getting married at the age of 29, which way did I go
from here? My wife, who was a native Frankfortonian, thought like the average
local citizen; that is, I should choose from the best of jobs available and go to
work. This did not say very much to me after having come from Mississippi by
way of Southeast Missouri where I had had experience on the cotton plantation,
the levy, railroad, and you name it, and I'd had experience on the job. In other
words, the sum total of all these work related experiences in my mind, along with
encouragement from a few well-wishers, led me back to school. Even though I
had to repeat some three subjects: organic chemistry, bacteriology and English,
this was a stepping stone to me when I looked back over past experiences, then
looked into the future which I must face. The answer came that I had no choice
but to make up my own mind, and double my determination and finish college.

My wife, being a native of Frankfort, joined those who felt that my decision
to return to college was a waste of time. But three years after I received my
discharge from the Army on October 17, 1945, my wife expressed her interest in
purchasing a home of our own. I wanted to stay in her grandfather's house a while
longer as it was rent free, and he had given us assurance that we were welcome.
Not that I had in mind to take advantage of his welcome for an indefinite period of
time, but I wanted to purchase our furniture over a period of time, maybe a year. I
had not finished college, but had only two years to go. I had planned to work at
two or three part-time jobs for a while until I had made up my mind as to whether
I would return to the classroom. Along with my janitor's job with the state, I
worked at a garage. Since my janitor's work was at night, I worked at the garage
during the day. This worked out very well for a while, but later I had to give up
the garage job due to a change in schedule at the garage. From there I went to a
local furniture store which paid better than the garage, but this didn't last very long
because handling the heavy furniture was a bit too much. From there, I went to a
store which sold clothing for women. During those times, persons would not be
accepted as a sales person only. If he were black, there were other duties attached

such as janitor, firing the furnace, and delivering merchandise. This included a variety of dresses that ladies requested to be sent to their homes on approval and picked up later those that were rejected. I talked over this proposal with my wife, and she was tickled because she could purchase ladieswear wholesale, and silk stocking during World War II were almost out of the question. But she could get extras because I was employed by the store. The question came to me, why, if I'm to become a salesman, should I do the janitorial work no other salesman in town did. Janitorial work and salesman too -- therefore, I refused to take the offer. I also worked at the picture show, as a janitor, for a short period, but grew tired of picking up popcorn boxes and all that went with the job between movies throughout the day. By the way, our son wanted me to keep the job because he got free tickets to the movies. I did some serious thinking; here I am thirty-one years of age, and where will I be in the years to come?

I've criticized those Frankfortions for not having gone to school, now here I am about to join the bandwagon, which meant that I would have given up all hopes and aspirations to be somebody. I went through all the above changing jobs and criticisms from my wife who was a native, and thought just as others in the community, that a high school education was sufficient for life. My wife did not want me to associate with those former classmates who frequently visited the college because of fear that they would influence me to return to school. She did not know that one of her friends who grew up with her here in Frankfort, never went farther than the sixth grade in school, but had a trade (refrigeration) and kept busy taking care of Franklin and all other adjacent counties with their refrigerator needs. I spent quite a bit of time with him. One Sunday afternoon during the summer of 1948, he came by our house and picked me up to go to Carlton, Kentucky to service a refrigerator. He knew that I liked to go for the ride, and he also knew that summer school was to have begun the following day. As soon as we got on the road in route to Carrolton, he said, "This time tomorrow you'll be back in school." I said, "No, I've changed my mind." He wanted to know why, and I said my wife doesn't want me to go. We had had a heated argument about it on the day before, and I went so far as to tell her that if she didn't want me to go, I might as well pack my suitcase and take off, because my going back to school would mean as much or more to her as for me. She took it so hard until I changed

76

my mind; and he said, "You told her exactly right." Immediately, I said "Earl, I'm going." He didn't believe it because I changed so quickly. When he dropped me at home, I thanked him for his advice and told him that I would register the next day. When I greeted my wife I told her that I had changed my mind again and would register the next morning at Kentucky State for summer school. I told her that I was going for her benefit as well as mine. We were not on speaking terms for a few days, but our doubts and fears soon passed away.

Not too long after we resolved our differences on the subject, we began telling what our friends thought about my decision to go back to school, and I was very much upset when she told me what the lady next door told her about my decision. The lady said to her, that before she would agree for me to go back to school, she would quit her job and make it as hard as possible for me. I immediately told her that I too had talked to this very same lady, because she had known my wife for a lifetime and she had a master's degree and was a former school teacher, church worker and public spirited citizen. This same lady had told me that she was surprised that my wife didn't want me to go back to school and that students were coming to Kentucky State from all over the country and after graduation were finding jobs or continuing with their education for better jobs beyond a four year college degree. Later on after I finished college, I was inclined to challenge this lady for having played both sides of our family's life against the middle, but after thinking the situation over and looking back over the cross sections of the Black population of Frankfort with regard to their attitudes about education, I changed my mind. If they were not convinced by this time of the value of an education, I would be losing time trying to convince them of the value of an education. And with the college located in their back or front yards and they did not believe, it would have been impossible for me to convince them of the value of an education.

A few local people received degrees from the college, but never put them to good use. I was thirty-eight when I received my degree, but tried to put it to good use. I shall never forget Mother's remarks with regards to my educational opportunity. She said many times, "Son, if you are fifty years old when you get it, you will have something to live with or for the rest of your life." Mind you, people did not live much older than fifty back in those days, but I believed in her and refused to settle for less than a college degree. My main reason for making a decision to remain in Frankfort was that I married a local woman whom I had to convince that education would pay, if one wants it to. And secondly, she wanted to remain in Frankfort as she had never lived any place else. Besides, this was a good opportunity for me to convince the neighbors that education would pay off, if used properly. As has been said heretofore, I've done every common labor job in and around Frankfort and many prior to my having come here, and I did well except the jack hammer job. Now that I recall, I was not too good chopping cotton on the plantations of Mississippi. Usually my job was to do the plowing, and as a rule plow hands could not weed the plants as fast as a regular cotton chopper. Between the time crops were laid by and harvest time, there were other farm related jobs to be done, such as harvesting hay or cutting cord wood. I also worked quite a bit at the gin in between times when we were near the end of harvest. Being the oldest boy at home, my chances for work were two to one as there were many jobs which required men instead of women.

❖

I shall never forget when I decided to return to college during the summer of 1948. While registering for subjects to take at that time, each subject had to be approved by the teacher in charge. While registering I heard that a faculty member, whom I thought quite a bit about, had gotten his doctoral degree while I was out on probation. When I went to his desk to get his approval to take the subject, I congratulated him for having received his doctor's degree. This was just like having spit in his face. He asked, "Who told you that I had a Ph.D. degree?" I could not name any particular body because it was talked among students in general. He finally said that he did not have a Ph.D. degree. He was approving my taking the subject under him, but if I was not ready, I'd better stay out of that

78

particular class. I hardly knew which way to go at that point because it was a required subject in my field, and that was the best time to take it. Therefore, I put special emphasis on that particular subject and came out with a B. Later I decided to ask another instructor who shared the office with him and overheard the conversation between the two of us. His reply was somewhat vague, but I came to the conclusion that he meant the professor was disappointed for not having received a Ph.D. But I couldn't understand just why he made such a remark to me as a professor talking to a student returning to school after having stayed out a semester because of failing grades.

I registered for summer school during the summer of 1948 and graduated in 1950. Flunking out was one of the best things that could have happened to me at that time. I knew what life was like without an education; I could see through those whom I started out with during the fall of 1937 who graduated in four years thereafter. They were employed in decent jobs. Having lived in Frankfort enabled me to keep in closer contact with those whom I started out with in 1937. They returned to Kentucky State on numerous occasions and told me about the job opportunities for one who had a degree. This caused me to double my determination to graduate. Money was no problem at this time as I was a service man, and the Federal Government was allowing servicemen to go to school on the G I Bill. I applied for aid, which I was granted, for summer school in 1948. I wanted a little job on the side but felt the need to put in full time in the classroom during the summer. And if things went well with me in the classroom during the summer, I'd consider a job to help defray expenses at home as my wife and a few other felt that I made a mistake in going back to school. I was real proud of my grades during the summer, but decided not to seek a sideline job until I found out just what my grades would be like during the fall. When I decided to seek employment for the second semester in 1948, I was reminded to get in touch with the Commissioner, and he gave me part-time employment as a janitor to help defray my expenses in school. I spent many nights up studying until sometimes two o'clock the next morning, especially with English, but it paid. I even qualified grade-wise to pledge to the fraternity, but had no money. I had the money during my second year because of my tailoring business, but no grades. Frankly

79

speaking, the money which I made during my second year, in 1938, got me in trouble with my classwork, and I was determined not to let this happen again.

Part of the cause for my having flunked out of college the second semester of my sophomore year was that I had a very poor background at the beginning having finished through the 10th grade in Mississippi. With my experience in farming, I thought I had it made, until after registration when I was faced with such sciences, as chemistry, bacteriology, genetics and other related requirements for one who majored in vocational agriculture. When I returned to the classroom during the summer of 1948, I went in with a double determination to make the grade, and as a result I graduated with the class of 1950. And all along the way I was reminded that my wife and a few of our native Frankfort friends watched to see my mistake, in their opinions, in going back to school. Sometimes we do things with reservations, but I never had any doubt as to whether I was right in my decision to return to school.

Career

After I graduated from college in June of 1950, I continued working as a janitor, full-time, along with other jobs, such as a service station attendant and at a local bank until August, 1952 at which time I was hired as a teacher in vocational agriculture for the farmers (vets) programs at Lincoln Ridge, Lincoln Institute, in Shelby County, Kentucky. I taught in vocational agriculture during the summer of 1952. I finished the unexpired term for the teacher who accepted a job in his home state. During the summer months, we helped the farmers with their farming programs and boys who were taking vocational agriculture in high school and had 4-H projects.

When I went for an interview for this job, I reported to the Superintendent's Office fifteen or twenty minutes early to find him there in his office alone. During our pre-interview conversation, I told him that I was not an "A" student, and in case that was the type of teacher they wanted, they might as well look for someone else. He paused for a minute before responding which led me to think I had said the wrong thing. Finally he said if I had told him that I was an "A" student, chances are there would be a question as to whether they would consider me or not. He said that "A" students didn't always make the best teachers. I got the job and enjoyed it for a month and a half. At that time, I was given another job in mid-September, in Scott County.

The first job I applied for was as a teacher in Kentucky. I taught seven months in Missouri before coming to college. I went for an interview in Shelby County, and of course, I was somewhat aware of how an applicant should conduct himself for the job interview, such as dress code, how to talk, and above all being on time. When I arrived for the interview, the first person I met was the County Superintendent who greeted me warmly. While waiting for the members of the Board of Education for the interview, I told the Superintendent that if they were looking for an "A" student for the job they would be wasting their time talking to me. I envied many of those who spent less time studying than I and went to class and made A's, while I had to struggle to make a C and sometimes had to settle for less. He paused for a minute, and finally came out by saying,

"If you had told me that you were an "A" student, it would have been a question as to whether we would consider you for the job; it takes more than an "A" for one to make a good school teacher." Many of those whom I finished high school with made better grades than I, but where did they go from there? When the interview was over, I was told that they would be getting in touch with me in case I was hired. Sure enough I received a notice within ten days that I was given the job.

It's your attitude and not your aptitude that determines your latitude.

After graduation with the class of 1950, I taught school four years in the Scott County high school system. In addition to working with the farmers and boys who had projects in vocational agriculture, I taught biology and science; the 10th grade class was my homeroom class. I spent a half day, on Saturday, visiting farmers and helping them with their programs; during the summer, when school closed for the summer, I spent five and one half days weekly with the farmers. Having been born and reared on the farm, along with my technical training meant much. I could never understand why it was so difficult to convince the young

81

black men to remain on the family farm with their parents beyond graduation and carry on the program from generation to generation. Instead of following in their parents' footsteps, they chose to go in other directions. Some were good, and others were not so good; therefore, many farms as well as farmsteads went down the drain and were eventually taken over by the bigger farmers.

While teaching, I had held on to my little, part-time janitorial job that I had since 1948. My co-workers at school teased me for having to rush home to Frankfort daily from Monday til Friday, to clean the floor and the restrooms in the State Office Building. In order to put a stop to that I reminded them that I was the only teacher on the staff who received a check from the Board of Education twelve months during the year in addition to the one hundred and thirty dollars per month. The janitors job was very easy and paid $160.00 per month for five days each week with annual holidays and two weeks vacation annually. I always looked forward to coming home each day after school and jumping into bed for thirty or forty minutes before time to go to the State Office Building to do my janitorial work.

The latter part of August, the agricultural teacher in Georgetown, Kentucky resigned to take a job in Cleveland, Ohio, and I was given first choice to take his job in Georgetown. I started in this job fulltime September 1st and taught vocational agriculture in the school system five days weekly along with visiting the adult farmers on Saturdays, assisting them with their farming programs, and supervising the boys with their farming projects. This enabled me to keep my janitorial job without assistance, unless I had to be off occasionally, which I did; but it worked out beautifully because I had reliable help. One of my immediate supervisors on my janitors job felt that I was making too much money with the two jobs, and I heard a comment he had made to one of my friends that he was going to put pressure on me so that I would quit the job as janitor. It got to me before he had time to follow through with his plan; therefore, I immediately took it up with the Commissioner, and he told me to forget it so long as the job was done that was all that was necessary. This was the same commanding officer who took me to Camp Shelby, Mississippi during World War II and told me that we should keep in touch if we survived during the war, because he wanted to help me to further my education. This worked out beautifully. Many of my co-workers would tease me from time to time when we planned our weekend activities because occasionally I could not participate fulltime because of my work as a janitor. My wife reminded me that I should call their attention to the extra $160.00 per month which I received as janitor. Besides, my job as teacher was twelve months per year, and the principal's was only ten months and the others (teachers) were nine months.

One of the oldest agricultural teachers in the state was in Lexington. He knew that I was very much impressed with his program and listened to his advice in many instances. I used his program, except he purchased a garden plower for teaching purposes only; but in addition to this purpose, I decided to buy the program. In addition to demonstrating it with students, I decided to use it for personal gains. I found that the closest place this plow could be purchased was Cincinnati, Ohio, 90 miles away, and it cost $750.00 I went to the First Federal Savings and Loan Association, where I had a savings of $250.00, and borrowed $500.00. I went to Cincinnati, Ohio and purchased the plower. They delivered it within ten days. In addition to using it as a demonstrator with the vocational agriculture boys, I advertised in the local newspaper that I would break grounds for gardeners. This brought more business than I could take care of on weekends. In fact, I found myself plowing a few gardens on Sunday. With each garden I plowed, I always left a sheet which contained my phone number and a suggestion as to what should be planted at given periods. This brought more business than I could take care of. In fact, when I purchased the plower, I thought my son would become interested in the business, and it would pay large dividends. But unfortunately, he was not interested. He had a paper route and had to be punished because he was more concerned about things that didn't pay. In fact, he would collect enough to pay his bill and forget the rest. Along with the plower I had the trailer on which to take the plower from one place to another. This convinced me that children are sometimes given too much instead of earning what they want. With this plower I was able to pay property tax, insurance, upkeep and many other bills. I finally sold the plower to a friend.

When my immediate supervisor in the janitorial work found that I had a job as a school teacher, he tried to get me fired. Apparently he thought I was making too much money. In fact, I felt that he at first didn't realize that I had finished college and was eligible to teach school. He told one of my co-workers that he was planning to see that I was released from the janitorial work, and the news got to me before he talked to the Commissioner. I got to the Commissioner before he did, and we discussed my situation. By the way, when I taught the adult farmers in Shelby County, I had to teach a class two nights a week, Tuesday and Thursday night. When I mentioned this to the Commissioner, he told me as long as I had someone to do my job on those nights, it was OK with him. This was disappointing to my supervisor, and he said very little to me thereafter. Later on, a month or two, office equipment came up missing in various offices, and they finally found that one of the night watchmen was taking it. Again, my supervisor told me that he thought I knew something about the situation, and further said that if this type of thing ever happened again, and he felt that I was involved, he was going to kick me in the seat of my britches. I told him that if he did he would be minus the foot he kicked me with. Janitorial service, like other jobs, consists of those employees who will take off at the drop of a hat, especially on pay day.

I enjoyed four years with the school system in Scott county (from September 1952 - June 1956), at which time the schools were integrated. All teachers involved had tenure except me; we had less than two hundred high school students, and eight teachers. These students could be absorbed into the city and county systems, with no problems as far as being overcrowded, without the teachers. Other teachers were quite concerned, even though they had from twenty to thirty some years experience in the profession. I received a letter from the Board of Education in March which stated that my service would no longer be needed in the Scott county educational system after June 30, 1956. This came to me as no surprise. As integration was taking place all over the country at that time, I knew it would eventually come to Scott county. A Miss Francis Boutin, now Mrs. Francis Collins, was Supervisor of Employment Services at that time with the Department of Economic Security, where I worked as janitor for eight years. She suggested that I should take a civil service examination. So instead of protesting through the NAACP as was suggested, I got permission to take off from school in May and apply with state personnel. Approximately ten days later, I took off from school, on Friday, and came to Frankfort and took the exam for social work about two weeks later. When I returned home, there was a notice in the mail that I had failed the exam. Immediately, I got on the phone and called the personnel office to ask when I could take the test again, and they wanted to know why I wanted to take it over. When I told them the letter stated that I failed it the first time, they said this was an error, and that another letter was on the way which stated that I was to come in for an interview on a certain day.

A few days later, I received the notice to report for an interview. I was somewhat concerned about the interview, so prior to the date for the interview I went to the office and discussed the situation with a lady who was in charge of employment services. Incidentally, I cleaned her desk five days weekly as janitor of the department. She immediately told me that this would not be a problem for her, the purpose of the interview was to find out how you meet and deal with people, especially those who come in need of help. She immediately called another lady in the department who had just recently had an interview, and between the two they set my mind at ease.

On the day of the interview, I reported to that office, and to some extent, I felt a bit more comfortable as a result of the meeting with those who had had a similar experience. When I went in for the interview, the lady who met me at the office for the interview was very pleasant. This relieved me of a certain amount of frustration, and as I entered the door to the interviewer's office, I saw two people with whom I was very much acquainted. In fact, I had been in on meetings with them on several occasions. This relieved me of all doubts and fears. A day or two after the interview, I met one of those who interviewed me on the downtown street. He asked me if I got the job, and I told him no. He replied by saying that he felt that I would be considered because of the way I talked and the way I was dressed. And he gave an example of a woman who came in for an interview who was overly dressed; she wore diamond rings, etc. The job which she applied for was to help needy people, and in case she appeared on the job of that nature, those whom she was to serve would feel out of place seeking help through her.

I became unemployed on June 30, 1956 with the exception of my janitorial work, until November 1, 1956. This is why I believe that it pays to expose oneself to the potential employer, beginning with the present employer, and if he doesn't see fit to promote you, someone else looking on will consider you for a better job. On November 1, 1956 I was employed as a child welfare worker in state government. Three months later the Department of Economic Security saw fit to create a new job in adoption in order to stimulate the Negro phase of the adoption program. Many Negro children were growing up in foster homes and becoming of age without parents or a home they could be identified with. And I was considered for the job. And mind you that one entering state government, as a professional employee, on the merit system, is on probation for at least six months. I applied for the job as Assistant Supervisor of Adoptions and got the job, but the salary would not become effective until I got off probation within the next three months. Six months was the minimum, but sometime it became necessary for this period to be extended. I was given an option to work in the new job at least three additional months, that is if I got off probation within this time, at which I would automatically get the salary with the new job. I was given the choice of either continuing to work in the new job for the salary which I was getting or take an examination. In case I passed it, I would be eligible for the additional salary.

I took the examination, but unfortunately failed the test by three points. But when the personnel director talked to me, I gained new life. He said that he knew a few people in the department who were higher than I, but could not make the grade that I made. I followed his advice and became eligible for the promotion, in salary, at the end of the six months probation. As I was advised in advance, the new job would require much travel, but the addition in salary compensated. It was a pleasure to travel throughout the state to inform Negroes about the adoptive program. I met many of my former classmates to find that many of those "A" students were mail carriers, police, and you name it, and that is what they were doing for less than they prepared themselves for in college.

When I was hired as a child welfare worker in 1956, I laid the janitorial tools aside and picked up a desk job in the same office I had once cleaned. At the beginning of my social work career, three months, I did much reading and attending conferences relative to the Child Welfare Program. During this time, I was assigned to the Franklin County Office. It was interesting to learn that there were a few people who came not only to learn about the program, but some wanted to know if they could get into the Child Welfare Program. Believe it or not, some were my classmates whom I envied in school because I thought they would become lawyers or doctors. But they were mail carriers, police, and jobs of that nature.

One day before I received my third check as a child welfare worker, I was promoted to the position of Assistant Supervisor of Adoptions. This was a newly created job for the purpose of stimulating the adoptive program for Black children, since many Kentucky (Black) children -- eager, active youngsters from tots to teens, and of all sizes and of all shades were in need of foster homes. We also stressed the Division's services to unwed mothers as well as the homemaker program.

I remember on one occasion while discussing the program with a group of public-spirited citizens, as usual, there were those who had questions, which we tried to answer, about the program after one of my college classmates wanted to know how to get into the Department of Child Welfare. This really shocked me because he was one of those persons I envied because he could pick up a book and get out an assignment in a very short time and go to class the next day and make an "A" on the exam while it took me hours to prepare for a "C"or less. Where I failed organic chemistry, he made 'A's," and while I was repeating the subject a year after he graduated, he returned to K-State to take an additional amount of chemistry in order to prepare for a better job with the Federal Government. He finally wound up taking a job with the local postal service in his community, where he finally retired. I know quite a few individuals who never went to college and retired from the postal service. I see nothing wrong with carrying the mail, but I do think there is a great demand for one who goes to college and prepares himself for better service, as well as better pay.

The law of Kentucky required that one under the merit system must be on probation at least six months prior to prominent status. Sometimes probation was extended for an indefinite period for one reason or another, and occasionally one fails to qualify for the position and is therefore replaced by someone else. I was appointed to the post of Assistant Supervisor of Adoptions and attached to the Central Office staff of the Division of Children's Services. I was given a choice to serve in the new position for six months or take a special examination. In case I passed it, I'd get the salary for the new position immediately. But in case I didn't pass the examination, I had to work in the new job for the duration of my probationary period for the same salary as a child welfare worker. The new salary would become effective immediately after probation. I took the examination and failed to pass by three points. But when the State Personnel Supervisor got through talking to me, I felt as though that I'd passed the test. The most encouraging thing he said to me was that he knew some of those supervisors in the department in which I worked could not have done as well as I did on the test. He suggested that I return to my desk and continue to do my job, and I would be off probation in due time. My salary would then increase to that of Assistant Supervisor of Adoptions, instead of Child Welfare Worker.

A great percentage of my jobs required that I visit local offices throughout the state. At one time my mother chose to visit us for a week; and it so happened that I had to be away during this visit for a week on my job. The closer it came time for me to return home, the more I wondered just what the situation would be like at home upon my arrival. Mother would be the first to greet me to tell me that my wife was upset with her because she felt that the wife should go to Sunday School on Sunday and prayer meeting on Wednesday evening. I told her that she shouldn't have done that because we had a very good relationship throughout our courtship and our most recent marriage (five years). Later my wife told me that my mother made her "mad as hell" about her church attendance, and I reminded her that she shouldn't let that upset her because she would be returning home in a day or two, and our home life would be back to normal.

As Assistant Supervisor of Adoptions, I was attached to the central office staff of the Division of Children's Services. This was an additional step towards strengthening the black adoption program of the Division of Children's Services. I worked on a statewide basis and met with black leaders to interpret the Division's need for homes and solicit their help in solving this very real problem. By these discussions, many who wanted a child learned the need for homes for black infants and older children. They also learned how to go about getting a child, and their responses were quite rewarding. Now that I've been retired, it warms my heart to no end to think of those children not growing up in institutions or foster homes because Black people had been helped to fully understand the need for adoptive homes after I took the program to them.

88

I worked six and one half years as Assistant Supervisor of Adoptions and later as an employment counselor. There were only five positions in this area of state government, and I was Handicapped Specialist, responsible for providing leadership and direction to the statewide program of services to the handicapped. This is the time when I began to receive respect from some of my former teachers at the college. One instructor (the one who was so disappointed because he failed to get his Ph.D.) invited me to talk to one of his classes with regards to my work and presented me to the class by saying, "This is one of the Governor's right hand men, who accompanies the First Lady on some occasions." And on another occasion a professor paid me a compliment by saying how proud he was of me, and how he and another professor went out of their way to help me reach the goal which I attained. These are some of the instances that led me to feel justified in establishing myself here in Frankfort.

Cast down your bucket where you are.

While working for the state as an employment counselor, on one occasion, I had an appointment the Foster Department, and while waiting in that office, I noticed on the wall a statement that read as follows: *"Good things come to him who waiteth, providing he worketh like hell while he waiteth."* At one period I remember having had as many as three jobs at one time, and during this time my wife and I attended a dance. She said I was caught in the middle of the dance floor asleep while others danced around me. My doctor told me many years ago, "You'd better make hay while the sun is shining" because when you reach fifty years of age you start going in the opposite direction. His statement reminded me of what Mother told me time and again as I struggled to obtain an education, and it seemed that everything worked against me, even time itself. She said, "Son don't be discouraged even though it takes you fifty years to get an education. You can live independently the rest of your life." But at that time, men didn't live many years past fifty; in fact, when one became fifty, he was considered to be an old man. But I listened to her, and now at age eighty-five, I wish she were here to see the progress I've made since that time, or since age fifty.

89

During my last nine years in state government, I assisted inmates from the Kentucky State Reformatory who were eligible for parole or release in finding places to live and work. I tried to keep in contact with the men I helped just in case they needed further assistance. All of this work and help was done in my spare time and at my own expense, and the New Way staff of the Reformatory made me the Concerned Citizen of the Month on January 11, 1973.

There is a destiny that makes us brothers, none goes his way alone, all that we send into the lives of others, comes back into our own.

On many occasions I took students from the Department of Sociology from Kentucky State University to the Reformatory for social events or panel discussions in an effort to help the inmates to prepare themselves to become a part of the free world again upon release. During one of our panel discussions, I suggested that the students introduce themselves instead of me doing the honor. At this particular time, the very first student who introduced himself started out by saying, "A few of you might know me, because I put up "X" number of years down here, and now I'm a junior in college at Kentucky State University. I plan to enter the school of social work upon graduation." This thrilled me to no end because it gave proof to those who were incarcerated that they too could have the same chance. One girl student fell in love with one of the inmates, and they later became husband and wife. One businessman whom I had known through the years was in real estate and was quite helpful. Not only did he provide dwellings, but jobs as well. I found that Frankfort's population was made up, at that time, of many who came to college as well as those who were paroled from the Reformatory. There were those who could not be paroled back to their hometowns due to the seriousness of the crimes committed. Of all the placements which I participated in, only two failed me. One was from Lexington, Kentucky. Since this was his first offense, we were able to place him not only in his home with his family, but in a local job as well. He came through Frankfort one Sunday morning around 2:00 a.m., on his way back to Lexington. He had car trouble and called me from a local service station to ask if I would stand for a fifteen dollar job on his car in order that he could return home. That I did and had to pay the bill later as he failed to keep his promise. A short time later I met him at the Greyhound Bus Station, and he told me that he did not intend to pay me. This was unbelievable because his mother died a short time before he was paroled, and the central office, here in Frankfort, called me on my job in Mayfield, Kentucky, as I did much travel on his request, to ask if I would return to the central office to take him to Lexington to view the body. I even took him by to visit his wife and newborn baby, whom he had never seen. But I never let this incident cause me to refuse others in need of my services. As they worked daily on the Capitol grounds, five days per week, and returned to the Reformatory on weekends, I kept close check on them when I was not out in the state, especially during my coffee breaks.

Another inmate with whom I spent much time was from Alabama, but was married to a Kentucky woman. They had one child. He spent five years in the Kentucky Reformatory, but was quite ambitious, outgoing, and admired by many who knew him. He spent much time in making plans for the day when he would be paroled. He was also a "ladies' man." I often reminded him that he was being watched as a result of his close relationship with the women. This practice caused him to be returned to the Reformatory for a few days. After his restriction was lifted, he was permitted to return to Frankfort and work on the capital lawn as before. As an employment counselor, I recommended him to the Personnel Board to take an examination which was granted. He took the test, made a passing grade, was paroled here in Frankfort, and became supervisor of the laundry for the mentally retarded in Frankfort Feebleminded Institute. Just about the time we thought he was making well on his job, he disappeared. A day or two afterward, he and another trustee were caught in a raid after having held up a store in the western part of the state. Each of them was armed with sawed-off shot guns, and were returned to the Kentucky State Reformatory where they remained until they had served their full term. This man told me that he was going to New York where he had relatives and friends. This was some twenty-five years ago, and I've wondered many times what became of him. He could do most anything he set his head to do. Approximately twenty-five years ago he made a wallet and checkbook cover for me which I cherish very much. Prior to 1937, the Kentucky State Reformatory was located here in Frankfort. This fact accounted for such a large number or high percentage of those released having decided to relocate here in Frankfort. I tried to keep in contact with the men I helped, just in case they needed further assistance.

FROM ACROSS THE BRIDGE

Chapter 3

There is a destiny
That makes us brothers.
None goes his way alone.
All that we send
Into the lives of others
Comes back into our own.

(Author Unknown)

FROM ACROSS THE BRIDGE

I have been retired from State Government twenty-three years as of December 31, 1996 and have worked harder since than ever before. Immediately after retirement I proceeded to do voluntary work at the hospital. It took me quite a while to realize how much it meant, not only to patients, but to those who came to visit the sick. One occasion I delivered flowers to a patient, on the fourth floor. As I entered his room I asked him how he was getting along. He said he was doing fine until he was told that his wife was also hospitalized. He further said that she was on the third floor, and I told him that I would go to that floor and find out how she was getting along and would return immediately and let him know her condition. Immediately when I left his room it came to mind that the intensive care unit was on that floor, and in case I went down to find that she was in the unit, it wouldn't help him for me to make this known to him. But I decided to play it by ear, and upon arrival to the third floor I found that she was not in the unit. As I entered her room, I found that she had flowers similar to the ones that I had delivered to her husband. When I told her this, I also told her that he said that he was doing fine until he found that his wife, or she, had been hospitalized. It didn't help his situation, but I had promised him that I would check her out and report back to him immediately. She told me to tell him that she was doing fine, just waiting for her favorite TV programs to be aired. I couldn't get back to his room fast enough to make my report, and when I told him what she had said, he proceeded to name the programs she was waiting for. I also found that occasionally we had visitors who were afraid to ride the elevators, or did not know what floor room "400" was to be found.

There is a destiny that makes us brothers. None goes his way alone. All that we send into the lives of others comes back into our own.

Knowing that, sacrificial love brings joy by giving of ourselves for others. We will find there's something to it when we do it. Faith is like a muscle in the human body; unless we exercise it, it becomes slack and weak. We need to employ our faith generously in virtue, in godliness, and in love of others. It seems most strange that we, sometimes, get our priorities confused and we give a helping hand to the fellow who needs it the least.

I am again reminded of the first car I purchased, a 1949 Chevrolet Impala. From childhood, I always wanted an automobile, but was determined to wait until I was able to purchase a new car instead of one already worn out. Many times I've seen those who purchased such cars stranded on the road because said cars had stopped. And it was common to find one who carried extra water because of a leaking radiator. When they reached the next pond they refilled; frequently they were stranded because of a flat tire, bad tire or tube, or both. I decided that I would rather do without a car until I was able to purchase a new car.

Therefore, I purchased my first car during the summer of 1949, a 1949 Chevrolet Impala. Seat belts were almost unknown; in fact, they were extra. I paid $35.00 for seat belts, had them installed, and bought a seal beam light with an eight foot cord to be plugged into the cigarette lighter in case of an emergency. My last Chevrolet was a 1968 Impala, and when I decided to trade it in 1972, I had in mind to continue with Chevrolet until I checked the Buick and found that the 1972 Buick LeSabre was just $500.00 more than the Chevrolet. Therefore, I was a Buick owner for many years. Eventually I drove a 1976 Electra 225. And after checking out the late models with all this computer business and inferior bodies compared with my older cars, I decided to put in a new motor in it and have the body redone. I was ready for the road. I've purchased many cars since 1949. All have been Chevrolets except the last two, which have been Buicks. My reason for having changed was I found that there was only $500.00 difference in the Chevrolet and the Buick. I bought my first Buick brand new in 1972. Believe it or not, in 1996, I'm still using the light which I bought in 1949.

When I bought my 1949 Chevrolet, I had just returned to school during the summer of 1948, and when I drove my new Chevrolet to class, one classmate told me that he heard one of my instructors make the remark that he hoped I'd be able to pay for it, as though I was not supposed to afford a new car. This was another one of my reasons to remain in Frankfort, to prove to a few college professors and those native Frankfortonians who thought I was silly going to college at age 25 and returning to the classroom in 1948 after having flunked in 1939. My motto has always been: *It doesn't matter where you were born or when you were born, but it's what's born when you were born.* From the day I purchased my first car, hence, I have been fortunate in being able to keep a reliable car as I trade every three or four years. I do believe that the rougher the road which one travels, the sweeter the success in the end.

We left Mississippi, where the white landlords told many blacks that they did not need an education, and that they would take care of them for the rest of their lives. It was unbelievable that I would land in a city where the college was located just outside of the city limits, and that I would find black people working as chauffeurs, janitors, cooks, maids, etc., whose landlords were telling them the same story. That is, "You don't need any more education; we'll take care of you the rest of your life. And if we succeed you in death, you'll get your salary the rest of your life." They fell for this idea, not realizing that the cost of living would not remain the same. For example, that type of employment paid, back in those days from $3.50 to $7.00 per week. Compare that with today's cost of living. Besides, a few lived with their parents who owned their homes, but were not able to keep their property up. Now that they are gone and their children couldn't afford to keep the property up, some have moved out. Eventually the city will become the owner. A few that retired, as janitors, etc., are found up and down the streets and highways picking up cans to sell. I know of some that retired from the state, whose parents left them a home, and they could not keep the property up with what they know in the way of a trade. They had no business working for the state in the first place. Even after having retired from the state, they could have gone home and operated out of their own homes, on their own schedules, and made more in a day then they made a month while working for the state.

On numerous occasions, I've been in on meetings where those who were chauffeurs spent much time talking about what we are going to do, or where we are going away on vacation. But when you learned the real truth, they were taking the people whom they worked for on vacation, and they did the driving, catered the parties, and you name it. And when they returned home, "after the vacation," we had to listen to their stories as to what they did while on vacation. They spent much time during social outings talking about where they were to go on their next vacation, when they were to trade cars, what they were to serve for dinner Sunday, etc. They called *Driving Miss Daisy* a vacation; it was for "Miss Daisy," as long as they did the service. They even bragged about their uniform which did look nice, but I learned long ago that looks, in many cases, are deceiving and do not meet the high cost of living. Also there were those who said if my boss precedes me in death, "I'll get my salary the rest of my life." They did not realize that the boss's death leaves a wife and family behind to be cared for; and yesteryear's salary (as they called it) does not commensurate with today's price of bacon and eggs. I like bacon and eggs too, but country ham goes pretty good every once and a while.

In all walks of life, I find that contacts are meaningful.

I still cannot understand the statistics on, unemployment, in this country. For example, ever so often the statistics are published on the unemployed, and many agencies publish ever so often that are "hiring." For example, not too long ago I ate at McDonald's, and on every tray on which the food was served was a mat which said "We are hiring." My mind went back to certain areas in our town where one can go at all times of day and find the same people standing on the corner, almost twenty-four hours a day. A few years ago, since my retirement, I worked for the Senior Citizen agency in our town, and as I was delivering a lunch to one of the shut-ins, I met a young man who worked at the Employment Office who had just left the corner where many of those, unemployed, hung out. He had told them that the agency was about to publicly announce the need for employees, and they preferred black applicants. He could not commit themselves as such to the public, and he felt that he was doing them a favor by telling them the story. However, they responded by telling him that the only way they would consider the job would be if he brought it to them on that corner.

I often think about times when my wife and I are traveling, especially in the fall when the farmers are harvesting their tobacco crops. Not only do they have signs indicating the need for employees to help during the harvest time, but the wages per hour plus one meal per day made me wish I was available for hire. I have asked many persons just how do they base their conclusions on the statistics on the unemployed, but no one has ever come up with an answer to satisfy me. Benjamin Disraeli (1804-1881) said, "There are three kinds of lies: lies, damned lies, and statistics." Even at my age, I could get a job. It might not be what I would like to do, but when I approach the clerk with a dozen eggs or a pound of bacon, they don't question as to where I got the money from. All they are interested in is the cost of the purchase.

When I go to church or attend social affairs, normally people compliment what I wear without asking where I purchased the attire. Even though it might have come from the Senior Citizens Center or the Good Will Store, if it's suitable for the occasion that's what counts; wear it. When I worked at the local hotel for minimum wage, I met guests from throughout the country. Many told me about places they had been where I could make more money as a Bellman than the manager of the hotel because of my approach to the guest. Even though this might have been true, the sum total of every job I ever had, whether I liked it or not (some I did not like), counted when the time came for me to retire.

There are people who refuse to work for minimum wages, and a great percentage are not worth minimum wages, but I have not only practiced, but preached that minimum wages are OK, if that's the best one can do at present. Accept the job and do the very best. If you can't get a promotion on that particular job, someone else will recognize your qualities and give you a better job. I am of the opinion that many of those that refuse to accept a job for minimum wages don't want to work anyway. In fact, I'm somewhat reluctant about recommending those who ask me for references. One person used me as a reference for a job without my permission. When I found that he had used me as a reference, it came as a surprise. When I was informed by the employer, she told me she tried to reach others he had used, but if I would recommend him she would forget about the other two references. And my reply was thanks, but no thanks, because he had many job opportunities and sometimes quit the job before time for his first pay check. His parents were surprised that I failed to recommend him because of our friendship, but that kind of friendship I don't need.

Those faithful few are responsible to see that the work goes on. I am reminded of an occasion about an employee who was a habitual tobacco chewer and used the trash can for a spittoon. I learned of his habit by unconsciously reaching my hand into the can in order to empty the trash that had to be forced out because of the spittle. When asked not to spit into the trash can, he suggested that I get a spittoon. I found that it was just about as difficult to keep clean as the trash can because half of the time he spat on the floor as much as in the spittoon. I find that any job one does should be done to the best of one's ability whether you like it or not. If those whom you are responsible to don't see fit to promote you in due time, someone somewhere will notice your good works and see that you get a better job somewhere. If I had a dollar for all the jobs I've had throughout life, I wouldn't have to worry about my future, money-wise. There are likes and dislikes on all jobs, even at home, but the sooner we learn to take the dislikes along with those which we cherish, the better our future will be.

I learned something on every job I've had that I find useful in my daily living. We knew nothing about minimum wages, or eight hour work days. I've worked until the sun went down on the farm. We went home to our daily chores before our day was ended. I've had jobs that I didn't like, but they were the best I could find at the time; and therefore, I had to continue until I could find something better. Regardless of the job, the pay, or what have you, if you have the proper attitude, that's what counts most. It's your attitude and not your aptitude that counts most. It's your attitude and not your aptitude that determines your latitude; I can think of many individuals who have degrees, and so far as they are concerned, they are not worth the paper which they are written on. My contention has always been, take advantage of every opportunity, and eventually things will come your way. Not everything will. For example, we might think we are worth more than minimum wages, and we might be. But prove that you are, and if your employer can't see that you are worth more, somebody else, some place, will see fit to hire you for better wages.

Study to show thyself a workman that needeth not to be ashamed of right fully divining the word of truth in honor preferring all men.

During the latter part of 1960, I became very bitter about the polluted politics in state government. In fact, it came to a point where the nearer Monday morning came the worse I felt about going to work. It really came to a point where I had to take medications to find relief. My plans were to tough it out five more years in order to qualify for full benefits. A friend reminded me of the fact that in five more years I may not be alive. But in the meantime as a result of those who retired, two or three jobs became vacant that paid more than mine. One I would have given anything to have been considered for. When this information was officially released, a memo was released to those who would qualify in the agency saying to apply if interested. I immediately submitted my resume. I went across the hall from my office to remind the supervisor in charge of employment for minorities (who was also black) of my decision, and he told me that I would not be considered because the man who was to make the final decision, who was white, had already committed himself to another white, who was less qualified, but they liked his dirty jokes. I walked outside of his office and invited him out to read his sign which read "Office of Minority Employment." I then proceeded to talk to a few whites about the job and how they felt about my qualifications for the job. One fellow co-worker told me that he didn't think I would qualify for the job, and another friend told me that I would qualify, not only for the job in question, but I would do better in the job than the person who made such statement was doing in the job he headed. After a period of assessment of the situation, I concluded that this fellow got the job as representative of employment for minorities because he could and would be controlled by the white majority.

It's almost impossible to win in a situation like that when your own race worked against you. Immediately, I figured that he got this job because he could be more easily persuaded than I because of having been in the state government a little longer and having known the personnel situation a little better. They figured it would be a bit more difficult to sway me as I knew the various jobs, and the personnel, through my janitorial service as well as professional. For example, during the late sixties, a student graduated from Kentucky State College who was very popular because of his record as a football player. He was employed in our department because of his fame, not only in athletics, but as a womanizer which qualified him to become closely allied with the personnel director who gave him prior consideration for vacancies in the department. This man came to the department at a time when the personnel director's record was questioned as a result of his unbecoming character on his job, especially when it came time to consider a woman for a job in the department. She probably got the job on the basis of not only how she looked, as she had to submit a photo, but how she talked. And in case she was considered for the position, the work didn't end with the close of the day, but continued after hours in his office, when no one else was around. It was known throughout the department that the personnel director would be terminated because of his character; I felt obligated to tell the new employee just what was happening as he was not only new on the job, but in the community as well.

This happened about at a time when blacks were being considered for better jobs than ever before in state government. Since he and I were from "down home," (he from Alabama and me from Mississippi) I felt that I had no choice but to inform him of just what was happening. *"Do unto others as you would have them do unto you."* It backfired on me; two days later three white co-workers and I were taking a coffee break and met the personnel director who stopped the other fellows. Of course being with them, I stopped too. He told them that they were running with a "no good fellow" -- George Simmons is no good. They did not know what was happening, and I didn't want to believe what had happened. In fact, I was flabbergasted. Here I was approaching a time when I would like to consider retirement and felt that I would be considered for promotion as my resume had already been submitted to the director's office for a vacancy within the department. In the meantime, I was trying to help a black brother along the way, who had betrayed me. I can't say that this particular incident caused me to not be considered for the job, but I'm sure it didn't help because the personnel office had a voice in the decision-making when it came to who got what job. And I also felt that I was obligated to share his, the personnel director's, opinion of me to my co-workers. After having talked it over with my wife, we decided that I should share this information with the fellows. I did, the next day.

When we lived in Mississippi, I thought the white people were against the blacks, to find later that our own race was against us more often than the whites. I've been in Kentucky many years, and unfortunately, I find that almost every worthwhile favor I've received came through white people. When I purchased the garden plower which cost $750.00, I had only $250.00 savings with the First Federal Savings & Loan Assn., and borrowed $500.00 from that agency and went to Cincinnati, Ohio and purchased the plower and paid off the loan on schedule. (I wished many times that gardening was a year round business, because I could make more money plowing gardens than on all the other jobs combined.) A few blacks in the community felt that my wife's grandfather co-signed my notes in order that I might borrow money from the loaning agencies. During that time, many teachers from the Kentucky State faculty could not borrow money from the bank without the president of the institution's signature because they had no collateral. Neither did I, but I never was refused my request for a loan.

After having proven to my late wife that one cannot fail with an education mixed with a bit of common sense, I think she still felt in the end, that I was traveling too fast in this congested society and would eventually be penalized. It sometimes seems necessary to me for a mate to go along with the proposed project so long as it is not too expensive, instead of saying, "I'm right, but you are wrong." I wanted to accept the offer to stay in her grandfather's house a bit longer while we built our finances a bit more, as he allowed us the privilege, rent free. But she felt that we were taking advantage of him, so we proceeded to look around for a house or a lot on which we could build.

It seemed that everything worked against us. After all efforts failed in the area we liked best, a friend and I went to Cincinnati, Ohio to talk with a lady who owned a nice plot on the outskirts of Frankfort, but this was a failure. She did not want to sell. One of the older citizens, a lady who lived just around the corner from where we lived, passed away. She had a daughter who lived in Anderson, Indiana; we proceeded to get in touch with her immediately in an effort to purchase the house. She gave her consent for us to buy the house; she also said that her mother would be glad if she could only know that we wanted the house.

She had lived alone, and anytime I saw her walking around town, I always offered to give her a ride and do little odds and ends for her. She priced it to us for $3200.00. While we were negotiating with the bank for a loan, they received an bid from a blacksmith who had a shop less than a block away for $3600.00. This would have been to his advantage, because he lived out in the country and had to commute to and from work daily. When I received the message, I told her that we would give her that amount for the house, and she told me that she would sell it to us for that price and would not go up another penny. When I went home and told my wife, I thought she would hit the ceiling because I agreed to buy the house for that price. It took much time to convince her that this was a good price for the house because it had apartments and the upstairs was already rented. She agreed, and I went back to the bank and closed the deal.

Our monthly payments were only $26.50. We moved in the downstairs apartment which had only a half bath, and the upstairs had a full bath. The upstairs apartment rented for $15.00 per month. We felt that the rent was too cheap. This was during the days we had a rent control law. I went to the rent control office and discussed the situation with them, and they advised that we would have to improve the property before they would allow us to raise the rent. We, my wife and I, decided to extend the kitchen back far enough to expand the bathroom downstairs into a full size bath. Not only did we make the kitchen larger, but put additional cabinets on the wall. We also built a utilities room in the back as well as the laundry room. When the job was finished, it cost almost a thousand dollars. I got all of the figures together and took them to the rent control office and they asked how much did we want to raise the rent upstairs. I told them that we were not sure as to just how much we should ask; and they suggested that we give them a few days and they would come up with a reasonable figure. A few days later they suggested they we should ask for $25.00 per month. This made us very happy because our monthly payments were just $26.52. Each month we only had to add $1.52 to our payment on the loan. This made us very happy because my wife had begun to think that we owned the house and lived downstairs, and the family or tenants upstairs had a full bath.

When we bought the house, I had in mind that this would be a steppingstone to something better later. The people were nice in the community, but this was the slums of Frankfort. A great percentage of the property was owned by a few who made investments for rent, and they kept it up just enough to satisfy the city fathers. Some of those who owned their property could not afford to keep their property up, and many of their offspring were not too concerned or couldn't afford to keep the property up on their income. Several families kept students who attended school at Kentucky State nine months each year, as there were only two dormitories on the campus. They also had high water problems ever so often, but didn't seem to be too concerned about the waters. They always looked forward to the day when the water came. Many had to move out, and when the water receded they would return to their homes and clean-up. Sometimes the rains came while they were preparing to move in, and they were forced out again. But they were very good neighbors. Everybody looked out for each other. Occasionally there were confusions, but most of this kind of thing was brought about by outsiders. Because of the above circumstances, however, property value was very low.

When slum clearance became a reality, many people were upset. In the first place, they were not able to get a replaceable price for their property which meant they had to purchase smaller houses which did not accommodate all of their furniture. Many had antiques that were irreplaceable. We became owners of two or three of said items. Besides, all of this caused many to relocate in areas that were undesirable, away from lifelong friends. A few went to an earlier grave because of the move. After having lived in a new location, in our first house we purchased, we too became victims of the move. But our situation was somewhat different. I had gone into the situation with the intention of using this purchase as a steppingstone to something better.

Five years later a house was put on sale just off the campus near Kentucky State college which was not in the slum area, and I contacted the owner as soon as the sign For Sale was displayed. She took me through, and afterwhich she told me that she wanted $12,000.00 dollars for it. The realtor told her that she was asking too much for it, but suggested that I go and talk to him. I immediately went to his office and expressed interest in purchasing the property. And by the way, my wife thought I was in the woods, squirrel hunting. I did, but didn't stay long because I wanted to talk to the lady about the house. And believe it or not, instead of going home to talk it over with my wife and change from my hunting outfit, I visited the owner and the real estate agency first. He told me that she wanted $12,000.00 for the property, but he had told her from the beginning that she had it priced too high. During our conversation, he got her on the phone and again told her that her price was too high and that he had a buyer for it, if the price was reduced. They finally decided that $7500.00 a reasonable price. When I went home, my wife was inquisitive about the hunt; because I came home without a squirrel and this was unusual. She was quite upset. I could understand her position because we knew that there was a question as to whether I would be retained as a school teacher when integration was to become effective in two years.

We then proceeded to discuss how I would finance this amount. I told him that we financed the first house through the Farmer's Bank, but had five more years to go before it would be paid for. Immediately, I mentioned the First Federal Savings and Loan Association where I had completed the payments for the garden plow. This might have been done through the Farmers Banks, but I thought it would be wise to make myself known to a variety of businessmen. We left the realty office and went to the First Federal. There we discussed the possibility of mortgaging the first house in order to swing the deal for the second house. The attorney for the Loan Association proceeded to get in touch with the lady who sold us the house. Everything seemed to go smoothly until the question came up as to whether there were other living heirs. The answer was no, but the agency would not accept this under five more years, for a living heir could appear within this period of time and the agency would be in trouble. They saw this was upsetting to me to no end. At that time I worked on two other part-time jobs. We had in mind to mortgage the first house in order to purchase the second one, but their lawyer said they could not take the risk of only one living heir to the house we had already purchased, and that we would have to make other arrangements to purchase the second house. But after five years, when we would have paid for the first house, and no other heir appeared within that time, we would legally own the house. This upset me to no end, and the President of the First Federal Savings and Loan Association saw that I was disappointed. He suggested that I should give them, that is he and the realtor, a little time to get together, and they would come up with a plan by which we could get the house.

He called me the next day to tell me that they had reached an agreement by which they could help us swing the deal and for me to come to his office immediately so that we might talk it over.

When I went to his office he told me that he and the realtor had decided to loan us the money. He said that I impressed him when I borrowed the money from the loan company and paid it back on time. Therefore, he loaned us $5000.00 and the realtor loaned us $2500.00 in order that we could get the house. I was so excited I didn't know what to do. And I had already been told, unofficially, that I would be out of a job the following June 30th. And when I went home and told my wife what was in the making of the purchase of the house, she had mixed emotions. She had a feeling that we were going too fast attempting to buy a second house when we had five more years to go before the first one would be paid for. But she went along with the deal. Our monthly payment on the second house $75.00, $50.00 to the loan company and $25.00 to the realtor plus the $25.52 on the first house which would be paid for in five years. And the agency and realtor got together and decided to take a chance hoping that there were no other living heirs to the property. The agency went $5000.00 on the property, and the realty went $2500.00. I signed an agreement to each of these at the loan company.

When I bargained for the house, I had in mind to rent it to someone on the faculty, at Kentucky State because it was conveniently located just off the campus. It had eleven rooms, but only one bath. This could have been easily solved, because I felt that teachers would be interested and could pay more for rent than the average citizen and less than they would pay on the campus. This would have made it possible to add another bath without a financial strain, but it just didn't happen that way. I paid $85.00 per month for this deal: $60.00 to the agency and $25.00 to the realtor.

And I had been told, by the way of the grapevine, that my employment with the Scott County Board of Education would end in June 1956. And as I have related, this became a reality in May 1956, when I received a letter from the superintendent that my job would be terminated June 30, 1956. When I told my co-workers about the situation, many suggested that I take it up with the NAACP, but this I refused to do because I had no tenure and felt that the thing to do was to look for another job. This was when I decided to take a civil service examination and subsequently became a social worker, which was somewhat related to my job as a school teacher.

But as I said, between June 30, 1956 and November 1, 1956, my janitorial work was all I had. And I had more financial obligations than this would afford. But for some unknown reason, I did not lose any sleep over the situation as I usually did. During this time, I was walking on the downtown streets and met the real estate broker to whom I had agreed to pay $25.00 per month on the second house we purchased on East Main Street. He asked me how I was getting along, and I told him about having lost my job with the Scott County Board of Education. I told him I had only $160.00 per month income until I could get something better. I also told him that I was hoping to get a job with the state as I had qualified by having passed the civil service examination, and was on the waiting list to be called at anytime soon. He told me to not worry about my financial obligation with him, and he further said that I had paid him enough on the loan, and that I should go to the First Federal Savings and Loan Association and tell them what he had told me and they would strike it off the record. I told him how much my wife and I appreciated what he had done for us.

This is the time I had decided we would rent the house, we were negotiating for, to teachers at Kentucky State College in order that we could meet our monthly payments. Immediately after we closed the deal for the house, we advertised it for rent. We felt that if we could rent it for $75.00 per month, the house would take care of itself. But three months passed, and no one seemed to be interested in renting it, so I decided that we had better move into the last house we purchased and rent the downstairs apartment where we lived for $35.00. This would give us $60.00 per month rent, and we could take care of everything. We immediately moved into this house, and rented the apartment downstairs, and everything worked out according to plans. We collected the rent and added $15.00 monthly which made everybody happy.

After having been married four or five years, we began to wonder if we could have our own child, by natural birth. I had turned 33, and my wife was 29; we made several visits to our family doctor in this regard, and he decided that it was almost impossible for us to have children. He did not rule out the possibility

106

of us having a child, but felt that at that time in our lives under the circumstances, we would be lucky. He then discussed the possibility of adoption, that is, if we felt that we could love an adopted child as well as one of our own in case we did have one of our own after the adoption. We took all of this under consideration, and during this time we visited my baby sister who had a child with whom I was very much impressed. He was three years old. When we returned home, we had a heart to heart discussion about this child, and my wife decided to go along with me so long as we adopted him legally. I always believed in helping the family, and in this case I felt that we were in a position to give this child a better education than she could, since we lived in a college city. My sister gave her consent, and we proceeded with the adoption. The child was placed in our home for at least six months during the adjustment period, after which we were permitted to consummate the adoption. We had only one bedroom, but we were permitted to allow him to sleep in the hall on the couch pending better arrangements within the near future. This too had made us more inclined to buy the second house instead of further expansion of the first house.

When we decided to move into the second house, we really did have a problem: moving out of a house which had only four rooms, one bedroom, kitchen and hall and one bath, into one which had ten finished rooms, eight downstairs and two upstairs with a huge hall in between. We then turned our attention to the used furniture store where we purchased according to the need over a period of approximately one year. First things came first, such as a bedroom suite for our son and other items which were purchased whenever or wherever we found the best bargain. The local merchants knew our needs as well as our financial circumstances; and therefore, when they got certain items through trades, they notified us of whatever they had. We purchased according to our monies. Within six months period of time, we purchased a bedroom suite for our son, Ray, and another living room suite, which gave us two living rooms up front, across the hall from each other. The hallway was approximately eight feet wide and extended within ten or twelve feet to the back of the house where there was another room which we converted into a laundry room. By the way, we had to increase the voltage of the electricity by 110 in order to be able to use our washer and dryer. Later I stopped by one of my favorite furniture stores and found a

107

beautiful dining room suite, table, six chairs, and sideboard of which the table was damaged when delivered from the factory. The furniture was two thirds of the original cost, and we paid for it on the installment plan. The damage was minor, so I got a can of maple furniture stain and went over it. One has to look closely to find the damaged spots. The company could have gotten more out of the deal, but saw we were struggling and did this as a favor.

Our friend who renovated the first house came to our rescue again; he renovated the kitchen, similarly to the one which he did downtown, and replaced the front porch concrete floor which had cracked beyond repair. This was an 8' X 15' porch. I crushed the worn out concrete with a sledge hammer, and we used most of the concrete as a foundation for the new. We had two flower boxes made, each five feet long and one foot wide for the porch, and painted them white, similar to the color of the house. We had plans to build a garage in the rear at the end of the driveway, but before we were ready financially, we found that the college was making plans to expand, and our house was to be included in their plans.

This news was exciting because we felt that we would get much more than we paid for the house if this was to become a reality, maybe enough to build the house of our dreams. Not long thereafter the college discontinued the Smith Hughes program which meant vocational agriculture would no longer be a part of the curriculum at the college, but would be transferred to the University of Kentucky. A portion of the 260 acre farm would be made available for housing for those who would be interested in building their own homes. This excited me to no end, but my wife was a bit reluctant about the situation. In fact, she always feared debts. I spent much time trying to convince her that we must take a chance if we ever expect to accomplish anything. Not too long afterward, the College Park subdivision was organized, and when I found that they were taking applications for all who wanted to become members of the organization, this too excited me. But my wife could not see the advantages of being in on the beginning; which meant those who came first had first choice for building sites and more. I became a nervous wreck, but to show additional emotions would not help the brewing controversy between the two of us.

108

What puzzled me most of all was we had made our last payment on our house six months prior to this time, and I felt that with all of our past planning being a success, she would be willing to go along with the deal. I could not think of anyone to refer her to for advice because she relied only on native Frankfortonions of her age group who had misled her in the past about some our plans which had worked out beautifully in our favor. I felt that jealousy on the part of these people caused them to have such attitudes towards our plans.

It seems most strange that one who is supposed to have an education would criticize another for striving to get an education. But many of our so called friends, kept my wife upset because they thought I was traveling too fast in a congested society for progress. But every day I was reminded of the late start I had as a result of having stayed at home twenty-five years trying to help our parents cope with the cost of living. It was not easy to start school in September and have to drop out, to work when a job became available so frequently that it took me twenty-five years to finish high school. Neither was it easy to live for less than a dollar a week during the seven months which I taught school in southeast Missouri in 1935. I should never want to see any more peanut butter or jelly. I ate peanut butter for breakfast, jelly for lunch and a combination of the two in the evening. I was often reminded that cavemen ate what they had to survive, and so did I.

In the meantime, while College Park was still in its early stage of development, another housing development, another subdivision, had its beginning a few months earlier. It was just early enough for one to see the type of houses were not what I had in mind to build and were more attractive to those people who were being relocated as a result of slum clearance. As I said, I sympathized with those who became victims of this situation, because many had never lived any place else and their homes were paid for. The inhabitants had accumulated much valuable furniture that could not be replaced and was priceless, and many prospective buyers wanted them, but did not want to pay what they were really worth. For example, one of my wife's friends had two captains chairs, and she gave them to us because she had no room for them when she was relocated, and she said the mailman wanted them, but didn't want to give what she thought they were worth. We were happy because they came at a time when we had moved into the house which had eleven finished rooms and not enough furniture to furnish even half of it. Another lady called me one day and asked me did I remember the table lamp that I had complimented on several occasions. I did, and she told me that she wanted us to have it. I could hardly believe what she was saying, because this is one of those items we could never afford. I think it is called a "Tiffany" lamp with different colors in the globe with lights in both the top and bottom or base. We had the chairs refinished, and they, along with the lamp, are priceless.

It was regrettable that those who were victims of the slum clearance had to sell their property for less than they could be replaced in a different location. Yet the city could not afford to pay more than the property was worth, and in the meantime property tax on said property did not commensurate with the cost of living at that time. I believe many of those who were relocated as a result of slum clearance went to an early grave because of this movement. One of those persons who talked from both sides of her mouth to me and my wife (about my decision to return to school during the summer of 1948) was a victim of this move, but she lived long enough after the relocation to see us move into our new location in College Park, where we built our home to our expectation. She was forced to relocate in an undesirable location in a house probably as old as the one which she was forced to leave because of the slum clearance. But I must say that she told me after the move that she was glad to see us in our new home.

During this time we knew that Kentucky State College, now Kentucky State University, was planning to buy our house which was two or three blocks off the campus, but we didn't know when, and we also felt that the property would sell for more than we paid for it. But it was to our advantage to decide which way we wanted to relocate as soon as possible in order to select a choice lot and decide just how we would pay for it. When my wife expressed her desire to go to Cherokee instead of College Park, I suggested purchasing a lot about three or four blocks down on East Main, and she was opposed to this. She said I just wanted to remain on East Main where I could sit on the porch and wave at those who passed by. I told her that I had talked to one of the local school teachers whose husband wanted to go to Cherokee, but she too wanted to go to College Park. She suggested that I talk to him, but by all means not to tell him that she sent me to him; and I did, but he still wanted to go to Cherokee. I felt that in case we, his wife and I, could win him, my wife would also change her mind. But it did not work. Therefore, I went to Mrs. Cherry, who owned the Cherokee sub-division, to discuss the possibility of purchasing a lot, to find that she had sold all that she had anticipated selling for that year (November, 1963), because of income tax purposes. But I should return the first of the year (January, 1964), and they would be able to come up with something.

This gave me a little bit more time to talk with my wife regarding the types of houses that were being built in the two locations. Those who built, knew the average family coming from the crawl had limited means with which to relocate. Finally, my wife decided to go along with me, and immediately we proceeded with our plans to select a lot in College Park and ways and means by which we should go about paying for it. We had anticipated paying for the lot out of what we were to have gotten for our house, but the University had not gotten to the point of even appraising our house. This caused us to put the cart before the horse in order to make sure to be able to get one of the two lots which we were interested in. So we went to the builder in charge and discussed the matter relative to one of these lots as we wanted a corner lot, and each of these were on opposite corners from each other.

As my wife often said, I wanted to relocate where I could see those who came into the community. And she was right because this is what I really wanted. It is impossible to describe my feeling towards the possibility of building my own house in the community where I once worked my way through school for $7.50 per month for my education, and also among those who were soon to retire as faculty members from the University where I was around their ages as a freshman. When I entered the college at age 25 in 1937, I was not recognized by many of those who taught because of this fact, and no one knew my parents. This would not make much difference because they were not among those of the big society; besides, I was not a smart student and had to work overtime in order to maintain a "C" which I failed to do for the first two years.

When I went to the builder to discuss these lots, he had me to know that on the one I wanted most, he had plans to build an additional house as a demonstrator. After having seen some three or four which had already been built, I felt that we would not want one of those because we wanted to build our own

111

house. When asked about the other corner lot, we found that it had not been developed on that side of the street, and he was not sure as to when it would be developed. He finally suggested that I take the situation up with Dr. Gus T. Ridgel, chairman of the project, head of the Business Department, and last but not least, from the same neck of the woods from where I came. I did not know him as he was younger, but he knew my family and came to Kentucky State College late. Therefore, I didn't realize just how much it meant for me to have become acquainted with one who knew my family and went to school with my sisters, after I had come to Kentucky. I was very pleased to know that he was close with my family, and he and I are fraternity brothers also. All this gave me much courage to go to him and ask for the lot. When I explained my reason for not having come to him sooner, he understood, and gave his consent for us to purchase the lot.

When I returned to the builder with Dr. Ridgel's consent for us to purchase the lot, I immediately discussed plans to pay for the lot within six months from that date, and he proceeded to draw up the contract as we had agreed. He said I could either pick up the contract the next day, or he would put it in the mail. I chose the latter, returned home, and told my wife the plan. Her grandfather, who was living with us at the time because his wife was in a nursing home, overheard the discussion and suggested that we let him pay for the lot as he was living with us. I left it up to him and my wife, and that was the final decision. So I called the salesman on the phone to inform of the most recent plan. He disregarded the installment plan, and we paid for the lot immediately, ($2,500.00).

Within two months after we purchased the lost, a friend (who worked for the University) heard about our purchase and came to ask if we would be interested in selling our house. I told him that it depended on how much it would sell for. He didn't know that we had to sell in order to build, but I told him we would decide how much we thought it would sell for and get back with him within a few days. I had learned that it was not good business to build until you sell because it might cause the builder to sell for less than the property would be worth in order to pay for the new house. This brought about another discussion between me and the wife. She was excited over the idea of us building our own home according to our specifications. We discussed the idea with a few friends, and they agreed with the wife that we should get as much as we could. They came up with

112

a figure of $12,000.00, and I disagreed because we purchased the house for $7,500.00 ten years ago without having made any major repairs. We did replace the concrete porch, put a roof on it, and painted it once during this time. In most of my dealings with others, I am reminded of what we were taught at home as children, and that is do unto others as you would have them do unto you. But that suggested price looked good to me, and I had to wrestle with it for a while because the house we had planned to build cost $24,000.00 And I had promised my wife we would build the house of her dreams. She had told me repeatedly that she did not like many of the houses we had looked at because she didn't like small rooms.

We had looked through many houses not only in Frankfort, but throughout the county and even went to Louisville, to the Fair Grounds where houses of all descriptions were shown. I was most impressed with the intercom system where the music could be heard throughout the house, at the front and back doors, and the patio, too. It took us at least a month to decide on a house, and we finally came back to Frankfort and went to the Frankfort Lumber Company. That is where we found the house of our dreams.

And at this time we got together on the price to ask for our house ($10,000.00). We immediately got in touch with our prospective buyer, and he was satisfied with the price. He wondered which loaning agency he should go to in order to get that money. I told him that we had dealings with the Farmers Bank as well as the First Federal Savings and Loan Assn. We bought our first house through the Farmers Bank, and the one in question from the First Federal. He chose the latter; and when he went to borrow the money he told them he wanted to buy our house. But before they went further with the plan, Mr. Karl Kagin told him that he had to talk with me before he committed himself. The next day I received a call from the First Federal requesting that I should come in and talk with them regarding the matter. When I went in I was referred to Mr. Kagin, and he reminded me that we paid only $7,500.00 for the house ten years ago, and asked if we had made any major improvement to the house during this time. Of course, my answer was no; he then said he would not be surprised if we didn't have termites, and before he would make a commitment to the prospective buyer it would be necessary for us to have it checked for termites. In case termites were found, it

113

would be our responsibility to get rid of them. He further said that he would loan the buyer only what we paid for it; and that it would be up to us as to the rest, $2,500.00, which we asked for the property. This required another get together between me and the wife. We decided to allow him to pay us the difference under a separate loan between the three of us. My wife suggested that he not pay it directly to us for fear he would be more prone to pay it through them than directly to us. We then got back with the buyer who was in accord with the plan, and he proceeded to talk further with the loaning agency to find that he was required to put up at least $500.00 in order to qualify for said loan. I talked to a realtor about the situation, and was advised to put this amount in the bank, in the buyer's name, and as soon as the deal was closed I could get my money back. This I did, and the next day I told another realtor what I had done and was told that this was illegal, and that in case it was found out by Federal authorities, I could get some time in Federal penitentiary. This really shook me up to the extent I could hardly sleep at night and wouldn't tell my wife because she was upset over many of the chances which I took. However, this was the only illegal deal I entered into not knowing what I was doing was illegal. It just so happened that he was able to close the deal early enough for me to recover the money in time, before it was known by Federal authorities what I had done was illegal.

The first of June, 1964, we employed a builder, recommended by the realtor who handled the business for the buyer of our house. We reluctantly accepted because of the advice given to us prior this time about the $500.00. At this time we had $10,000.00 cash from the sale of our house, and borrowed $14,000.00 from the First Federal Loan for which to build. I could hardly believe that my dreams were about to come true. During this time, I began to notice that my wife was not responding as I thought she would have as a result of our success. She became irritable. For example, we made a weekend visit to some friends who moved from Frankfort during World War II to Dayton, Ohio and discussed our plans with them. By the way, such friends as these and others from our area had moved to Dayton during the war and purchased homes, and this was much encouragement to me. When we visited this family and others who migrated to Dayton, from Frankfort during World War II to work in the defense plants and other related industries and purchased beautiful homes, I was determined to do

114

likewise. These were people, like myself. I decided if they can do it, I can too. One friend who impressed me most was a delivery man at one of the local drug stores and did electric work, on the side. He decided to go to Dayton as an electrician, but his wife refused to go. He went to Dayton, thinking that she would change her mind and join him at a later day. But this did not work out the way he expected; he gave her an ultimatum of which she disregarded. After which he focused on looking out for number one. He was well recognized in his profession at the plant, and during the time while there he began his plans beyond war time. He finally went into the real estate business in which he was a success and later got married to a lady who went along with his plans, and they made well. For a number of years I've wondered just why men proceed women in death in many cases. And this just might be the answer, we are sometimes faced with decisions that are proven to be right, and therefore, are forced to go against not only our mores but our parents as well. This man was a success, and the reason I used past tense is because he has since deceased and his former wife also, but she had to struggle in order to make ends meet after he left. My case was somewhat similar; but instead of a wife, whom I desired, but could not justify or qualify to propose to at that time, I was forced to leave home in order to prepare myself.

As a result of the conversation about our progress with our building plans, we left Dayton earlier than we had anticipated and returned home without having said one word to each other. And for one reason or another she lost her job with the state. She got to the point she couldn't read, such as looking up her beautician's phone number to make an appointment to get her hair done. She wanted to return to her job, but the employer refused to accept her for some reason. We went job hunting, and I found that she could not fill out an application for a job. We were quite fortunate in having a friend who gave her a job with the state in the laboratory.

During this time, our friends from Dayton paid us a visit, while our house was being built, and the wife expressed reservations about me building a house of this quality knowing that my wife was not well. Her husband left Frankfort after having lived here all of his life, gave up his job here as a school teacher, and went to Ohio for a better job. During this time they purchased their first home, in Dayton, and I wondered if they ever paid for it after many years. I'm sure its value

115

was less than the one we were building. I was very much excited about this house because it met with my wife's approval, and it gave us a chance to prove to the average resident of Frankfort what could be done, especially those who turned thumbs down on me for having entered college at age 25.

After we signed a contract with the builder in 1964 to build our house, from that day until the house was completed, I doubt that a single day passed without me visiting the site until the house was completed the latter part of October. The builder wanted to select the lumber company of his choice for the building materials. His reason for this was that he thought the lumber company that we chose was too high, comparatively speaking, but I told him that we liked the company best. Our reasons for the selection were that they used black employees, and his did not. Knowing that I was responsible for three additional houses in this community for his having gotten contracts to build at the same time he built our house, he was compelled to listen. During my constant visits from day to day, I found that he was prone to short change us in a few instances, such as moving the third, or half bath downstairs since we wanted a full basement, with poured concrete instead of concrete blocks and a mantel piece (over the fireplace downstairs). On one occasion during my routine visits, I found that the stone mason laid the stone above where the mantel was supposed to have been placed. When I reminded him of that fact, he apologized and said if we didn't mind, he would cut into the stone and put a mantel in to match the wall. But he didn't do that; the plans called for a roof over the stoop at the kitchen door, but he failed to do that. The picture window in the living room was supposed to have been almost twice the size of the one which he had installed, and we demanded that he install the window according to the plan. He was supposed to have completed the house by noon on Saturday in order to pay his employees, and we found that we were short two doors, on the outside (for the kitchen and the front, as we have central air). He rushed to beat the clock in order to complete the job and get paid.

While he was doing this, I went to the First Federal Savings and Loan company to okay the job so that he could get his money. While waiting for him, the President of the loan company asked me who did he owe out of the check. Of course I did not understand; I thought he had reference to those who worked for him on the house, not realizing that he had obligations with both the Frankfort

Lumber Company and the interior decorators. Therefore, while waiting for the builder to appear to collect, the loan company wrote three checks, and we could tell that the builder was disappointed when he came to collect. I was told that if the loan company had paid him the total amount owed, he would probably still be paying these other participants.

About a month after we had moved into our new home, I met another builder whom I knew very well, and I told him about our experience with the builder. He suggested that we allow him to come in and look the situation over. When he came, the first thing he observed was that we did not have a single ventilator in the entire house, and he took a look in the attic and found that the roof did not have sufficient support. That is, we needed at least eight additional 2 X 4's as braces, especially during the winter when, in many cases, we would have heavy snow. With the lack of sufficient support, the roof would cave in or crash. He further said that I could do the job, and after he explained how it should be done, I purchased the material and did the job myself. The builder's brother who participated in the building came and made the necessary provisions so that the house would have proper ventilation; otherwise, within two or three years the roof would have deteriorated as a result of the weather. We had quite a bit of stone (Bedford) left and had plans to use it around the house, for such as a barbecue pit, etc. And luckily I was at home when the builder sent one of his men to get a portion of the stone in order to complete another job he had going in the community, and I refused to allow him to get the stone. He was strictly a con-man, if there ever was one. He knew many of the black people in the community, and he made a point to employ two or three blacks, locally, who were also builders in order to get as many jobs as possible in this community. He even asked to appear on a program in the black church at the time he was building our house in an effort to impress as many blacks as he could in order to get as many jobs as possible during the development of the community. He impressed many, and did get three of the houses that were being built at that time. One occasion, two of us whose houses he had under construction at the time had some questions about our houses, and we visited him to discuss our situation.

When we arrived at his house, he told us that he had been out buying cattle and wanted us to know that he purchased both Herefords and Black Angus, that is black and white in order to give the impression that he was for integration. He even said in some way during the program which he participated in at the black church, that he cherished our friendship very much, and this went over in a big way. One of my questions was that he had promised us a cedar closet in the hall between the bedrooms, or convenient for all three of the bedrooms and the bath. The master bedroom was supposed to have been sound proof, and he tried to convince me that when he put the insulation between the walls that automatically made it sound-proof, even though the door was not insulated properly in order to make it soundproof. The plan also called for a folding door between the dining room and living room, and he had placed a regular door between the kitchen and hallway which leads to the living room. This also was not in the original plans, but we found later that this was cheaper like other similar things he did like the cedar closet that we never did get.

We had two motives in moving the half bath downstairs. First, it made it convenient for one coming in from work on the lawn to take a bath before going upstairs. And secondly, it gave us a chance to display the three antique chairs along with the captain's chairs in the area adjacent to the kitchen along with a round table which we purchased to complete the set. It was quite interesting about the table which had several marks left in it. I thought they should be removed, until the upholstery company emphasized the importance of leaving them as such. When it came time for us to select colors for the two upstairs baths, that is tubs and sinks and stools, my wife said just make them both white. The builder said that was unusual for women; and I told him that she was not well. He told me that he built a house for a couple, and before it was completed the wife passed away. I didn't tell him that my wife had been upset from the beginning because she feared debts. I decided that the one in the master bedroom should be pink and the other one white. Many times during the building of the house and after we moved in, she mentioned that she would not be able to keep up the payments in case I should succeed her in death, and I constantly told her that she could rent to someone. I mentioned some her friends, which might not have worked out as well as it would have if she would rent to someone else, mind you, the monthly payments were only $115.00 per month for twenty years.

118

Many times the thought came to mind that had if we been away from many of my wife's lifelong friends who thought as she did, things would have been better for all concerned. Knowing that what I was attempting to do was good for the two of us, I continued with our plans, and the good Lord saw fit for us to enjoy our new home together nine years, eleven years before the house was paid for. One of her close friends, whom I used to admire very much thought she would be my next choice, but she got married to her childhood boyfriend, who after having finished high school, became a chauffeur and died before my wife. She knew that I was interested in her way before my wife and I were married; not only did I like her as a person, but she graduated from Kentucky State College in music. I felt that if she and I could get together I could fulfill my parents desires, even though late, in taking music.

Our house, if placed on the market for sale, would cost at least one hundred thousand dollars, and it's been paid for six years, October 30, 1990. As I look through my "rear-view mirror" of life, I can see a number of those people today as they saw me then. Likewise, I see those who made fun of me for having gone to college at age 25 as they still work for the second, third or even fourth generation of those families that they have served down through the years. Those whose families owned their homes were somewhat fortunate to succeed their parents when it came to ownership of the home place, but the homesteads are falling apart for the lack of upkeep. They are not able, either intellectually or financially, to see the value of keeping their property in good repair; therefore, chances are that they will be forced to move wherever they can regardless of circumstances because they cannot afford decent housing. When it comes to living in housing projects, things are quite different as a whole. You might prefer a different setting, such as location and neighbors, but you have no choice due to the lack of money. I have wished many times that many of those who grew up with her had lived to see how well I've done. Not only is the house paid for, but I've been able to keep it up to par from year to year.

This thrilled me very much to know we were building among many of those faculty members who knew very little about me except that I was the oldest member of the class and from a very poor background in high school. Plus none of my family was known in society. One faculty member, who was away at school in the summer when we and others were building, came home during the time and told another faculty member who was building at the same time that he could not build the type of house we and others were building at that time. He had the lot but knew a very little, if any, about building or how to go about preparing to build. I am sure he was reminded of the fact, as he looked at our structure going up, of how he ignored me in the classroom. But thanks to God that we built the house and paid for the loan on schedule. We borrowed $14,000.00 from the First Federal Savings and Loan Association for 20 years; $115.00 per month. We paid it off on October 30, 1983, fifteen days after my 72nd birthday.

We moved into our new home as soon as it was finished, and the Collins' took over the house which they purchased from us. Within a year's time, Kentucky State University purchased the house from them for $36,000.00 and gave them $500.00 to move themselves. At first I wondered if we should have held on to the house and waited a while longer to build, especially after we got the lot. But when I looked the situation over and considered how fortunate we had been in our dealings up to this time, it was not so bad after all.

It's impossible to win every hand regardless of what the game might be.

This plus other things that have come my way through the years made me feel justified in letting the house go to my friend who was, as a result of the deal, able to buy a much better house in a better community. What goes around comes around.

Our house is known as "THE WARWICK," a spacious home of pleasing lines, and universal appeal: living room, 21' X 12', dining or family room, 14' X 12' 6", kitchen 14' 8" X 9', bedroom 16' X 12'; bedroom 12' X 12'; bedroom 10' X 11'; two baths, with linen closets; hall with coat closet between living room and garage; garage, 290 sq.ft., including storage. While the house was being built, we shopped around for furniture sales, especially for the master bedroom. We had three antique kitchen chairs, and we tried to have a fourth one made from a local furniture company that made furniture, but to no avail. Our reasons for the fourth chair was because we decided to move the third half bath downstairs and use the space provided of the kitchen as a kitchenette. We discussed this with the

120

furniture salesman, who could not make a chair to match our chairs because it would be almost impossible to find wood to match said chairs. But we found his furniture was as reasonable in price as we could find any place. It might have cost a bit more than other companies, but the quality was superb. So instead of replacing the chair, we bought five pieces for the bedroom from him: queen size bed, dresser, chest of drawers and two night stands. Later we went back to this company and purchased a wash stand to accommodate a set which we had to be placed in the hall. During the search for furniture, we found a round table that was a perfect match for the three chairs and used the captain's chairs with the set.

I never heard of patios until relatively late in life. Similar to showers we always referred to showers as rain. But now we have two and one-half baths, with showers in each. The half bath is in the basement, for convenience. When I come in from the outside, after having worked on the lawn I can shower before going upstairs. Not only do we have radios in our bedroom, but in the other two bedrooms as well as in each bath, upstairs. We also have the intercommunication system, which makes for convenience for radio throughout the house. It saves steps and energy to communicate throughout the house. There was a time as I said, during my courting days, when I was quite pleased when I visited my girlfriend and some member apologized for having to use the lamp to go into some other parts of the house for one reason or another. This gave us, me and the girlfriend, a chance to do a little kissing. We now have five lights in the master bedroom plus two in the bath, three in the front bedroom, two in the middle bedroom, three in the guest bath, one ceiling light in the dining room, which contains five globes, seven in the living room, four in the kitchen, six in the den, two in the shower (off the den). A full basement consists of the den, a huge storage compartment, four lights and washroom and deep freeze which contains several items that should be discarded and the third part for Christmas decorations, ironing board, for pressing clothes as well as breakers, instead of fuses, which is a big help. We also have three lights out front. We no longer have to clean the lamp chimney or put kerosene in the lamp in order to have light. We don't have to worry about replacing fuses, the system is controlled by the breakers. Two lights are in the garage, a refrigerator and a deep freezer in the basement which reminds me of times on Squirrel Lake when we needed ice for special occasions, like

121

church affairs. We have lights in each switch throughout the house so that we no longer feel for the switch which causes the need for covers over the switches in order to prevent soiling the wall in search for the switch. In fact, one can go from place to place throughout the house without turning on any light, by following the automated light which shines in the dark and goes off when the lights are turned on.

On Squirrel Lake, we met the ice truck out on the road, only on Saturday, as this was the schedule in that area on which he ran. And if the ice was to have been kept for a day or two, we covered it with sawdust and wrapped it with an old quilt or something of that sort. It came in blocks, twenty-five, fifty or one hundred pound blocks and was carried with ice hooks and separated with an ice pick. In case one lived a distance from the route on which the iceman came, it was necessary to hitch mules to the wagon in order to transport the ice to the designated place. We no longer have to meet the ice man out on the road in order to purchase blocks of ice. Our ice is supplied through the ice maker in the kitchen. Foods are kept in the freezer for preservation.

We also have the automatic garage door which is controlled from the cars. And when I say cars, I mean each of us, my wife and I, have our own cars and automatic controls for the garage door. Speaking of closet space, ours is similar to the full basement. We have double closets in not only the three bedrooms, but in the hall between bedrooms, in the living room, as well as in a huge linen closet in the guest bath. Speaking of the baths, we have two that are white and one in the master bedroom that is pink. We have shower curtains of various colors.

This reminds me of our first visit to Dayton, Ohio with friends who were originally from Frankfort. This is where I had my first bath, under a shower. I was overly excited when I got out of the shower. I noticed that there was quite a bit of water on the floor beside the bath tub, but could not understand why. Later I discussed it with my wife to find that I'd made a mistake in not putting the curtain inside of the tub instead of outside. This embarrassed me to no end, but the friends never mentioned this incident to me.

Our reason for bringing the third bath downstairs was because we decided to have a full-size basement with poured concrete, and with the family room downstairs. There we installed the old mantel piece which I was very fortunate in

122

getting when the old slave house was demolished. I had it refinished, and it makes a beautiful setting, especially to me because I admired not only the mantel piece while staying on the farm as a student, but the entire building. And I never dreamed that I would ever be asked as a third party on a committee to select something, for a keepsake, for the University, and that the mantel would be mine as a result of the other two members of the committee deciding on a window frame.

The conversion of the two hundred and sixty acres of land into an extension of the athletic program for the University and a portion for those who wished to purchase lots on which to build their own homes meant much to me in more than one way. In the first place, I am the oldest resident in the area as a result of having lived in the area since April 1937 as a student. Secondly, I can appreciate the changes more than those who came in later. There isn't a square foot of ground in this two hundred and sixty acres that I don't have certain memories about: some are good, and others are not so good. For example, there is a spring in the bend beside the railroad track where we kept a cup from which we drank the good old spring water to quench our thirst. Not too far from this point is the old barbecue pit where we roasted meats of various kinds for the agriculture department. There's the poultry house where I gathered the eggs and sold a few, both eggs and chickens for show fair. One occasion I delivered two bushels of corn to a nearby farmer, but then promised myself that I would not repeat that. I had no idea how heavy two bushels of corn could be on one's shoulders, especially when it was an illegal deal.

Some people ask me how I know so many people, and this is part of the answer: I've worked on most jobs in Frankfort, before and after I finished college, and even since I retired. The most intriguing job was to work with the handicapped for one year, but they allowed me to work only one year because of my income. Not only did the job pay well, but it gave me a chance to continue in the type of work which I retired from as a handicapped specialist, where we placed special emphasis on seeing that all handicapped people were considered by the potential employer and as many of those we felt could be eligible with additional training. I even worked with the Revenue Department five years, seasonally, approximately five months each year for five years. My reason for terminating my service with them was because I wanted to work fulltime throughout the year. They had no such vacancy at that time; so I went from there to the senior citizens whom I enjoyed and remained with that agency two years and four months. But they only employed me one-half day five days per week.

In the meantime, we who worked there had access to clothing that was donated to the agency and vegetables that were donated to the agency from the Governor's garden during the summer. I remember on one occasion there was a lady who lived out in the county whose husband had passed away, and I transported her to and from the center daily, five days per week. As a result of having lost her husband, she decided to move into a smaller apartment; therefore, she had to dispose of some furniture which she did not have room for in the new apartment. One day as I went to pick her up to take her to the center, she told me about the couch. She said she had advertised in the local newspaper, but no one seemed to have been interested in it. I asked her how much she wanted for it, and she said that she had advertised it for $150.00, but it seemed as though she would have to reduce the price to $100.00. She further said that her husband paid $120.00 less than two years ago. I asked her if I might see it, and when I saw it, I asked her if she would let me have it for $100.00. She said she would, and I bought it along with an extension metal ladder for $50.00. I have much clothing, such as suits, sport coats, extra trousers, overcoats and hats that were my size already cleaned. These things along with contacts made on the job should be considered when it comes to wages on the job. I worked at the Capital Plaza Hotel four years for minimum wages, but I guarantee that this was double, at least, in tips as well as contacts.

A good name is better to be chosen than great riches.

During the summer of 1950, I worked at the Farmer's Bank as a messenger for minimum wages. During this time, the bank was renovated, and among the gifts from local citizens was a plant, that evidently no one knew its value. Therefore, after a period, it was dumped in the trash, and I took it home. My wife, who thought she had a "green thumb," took it and nourished it through the years, and as a result it is among those items which we cherish that is displayed in the family room along with the mantel piece. It reaches the ceiling, and to me, it's priceless. The Bible says,

They that wait upon the Lord shall renew their strength, they shall mount up with wings as eagles, they shall run and not be weary, they shall walk and not faint.

I recall on one occasion I was appointed by a civic club that I belonged to, to represent the club. When I arrived at the meeting, I found that it was a luncheon meeting, and I saw there were set-ups for their own, but not me. I participated in the discussion at hand but did not eat; this was before integration was a reality. When I returned to the next regular meeting of the club to make my report, I told them that they were not expecting me to the meeting, and therefore did not prepare for me to eat. Some native Frankfortonians made fun about the situation, and I told them about some of my experiences in coming up in Mississippi. We sometimes had occasions where we went to a landlord's house in the wagon probably to pick up something or deliver something and happen to arrive at mealtime. We'd sit outside in the wagon and wait until the meal was over, and sometimes we were favored with a sandwich which was brought out to us, not in a plate but in their hands, "hand delivered." So this was just another one of those things. These are the kinds of things that made me more determined to finish college. I thought for a long time that this kind of thing happened only in the deep south. The older I get the more I realize that *you never get too old to learn.*

Many times I look back at how I came here and at the various jobs I held in order to get an education. I become disgusted at the opportunities the natives have had and blew them. The more I see, the more I feel that I did the right thing to "cast down my bucket" here. There are those whose parents died and left them not only homes that were paid for, but cash as well. And today the homes are deteriorated, and they have no money to keep them up. Therefore, some are paying rent. There are those who purchased expensive automobiles, town cars, and work as janitors and maids, etc. I am reminded of one couple who have both a Cadillac and a Lincoln Continental, and the house in which they live is not worth the price of either of the two cars. They added on to the house after a period knowing that the high water comes ever so often to cause them to move out. And when the water recedes, they take time off their jobs, and go in and clean the house and move back until the next time, not counting the cost for moving in and out. But they both work for the state, which means that they are not always sure of a job when the administration changes.

At one time I felt that it was good for children to pattern after their parents. Even though their parents may mean well, I'm not sure that this is a good pattern for children to follow. We must also realize that when we depend on the government to relocate us, we are forced to accept what they offer whether we like it or not. We sometimes wonder why things don't work out as we wish, but the answer comes later. For example, we tried hard to invest in property in four different locations; two were houses and the other two vacant lots on which we wanted to build. All failed. The answer came later that this was not the ideal place not only to build, but also to live because as a result of the slum clearance, it would not have been suitable. I had one person who moved into Cherokee to say that he would never have had a bathroom had it not been for the slum clearance. The homes are better, but the pattern of living remains the same. One can hardly pass through the street for cars parked on either side of the street. Some need mechanical work before they will move. An additional location where we tried but failed, was in similar condition as the others. It took years before the answer came as to why we failed in these endeavors. Now that we are happily located in College Park for almost twenty years, I look back and see just why we failed in all of the previous efforts. We built the house according to our specifications, even though cheated in a few minor instances. We look back and consider how fortunate we were through it all. In the first place, even though late making a final decision to purchase the lot, we were fortunate in purchasing a lot where we could greet those who came into the community. This community is somewhat different than those which we first pursued. For example, the majority of those in this community are retirees, mostly from the University.

As we go from place to place, I am often reminded of things that happened during my tenure as a student in this area, such as milking the cows by hand, instead of with milking machines. We tilled the soil and took care of the rest of the livestock, as well as the fruit and vegetables. We supplied the college with a great percentage of its foods. We walked to and from classes from the farm. When I came here, I wore long underwear during the winter, while others, on the farm wore regular underwear throughout the year. As I have said, this was somewhat embarrassing to me because our laundry was done on the campus by girls who were working their way through school. I did not want them to know that I wore long draws (LFD's) as they were commonly called by students (long funky draws); therefore, I did my underwear myself on the farm. Not having had the proper equipment to do the job, they became dingy, and this problem along with changing them on Tuesdays and Thursdays at the gym, made me quite unhappy. I finally stopped wearing my "LFD's, " but I refused to get rid of them. They come in handy during hunting season on a real cold day.

Now that I take a second thought, it may be that my ability to kill a rabbit, occasionally, might have played a role in my having become acquainted with my unexpected-to-be wife, when my wife died in 1973. During their having worked together, my wife found that she liked rabbit too, so she suggested that I take her a rabbit after a day's hunt. We never know just what the future has in store for us, which is sometimes in our favor. When my wife constantly told me certain things about the unexpected wife-to- be, it gave me an idea that this should be my next wife after my wife died. I talked the situation over with my mother, as I always did, and she encouraged me to proceed, because as she stated, "You are too young to spend the rest of your life alone, that is, if you want to get married again." I was 62. And the next idea that came to mind was just how would I, or we, cope with public opinion because there would be some who would think I was looking at this lady before his wife died. I also talked the situation over with a fellow co-worker who was a minister, and when he told me that his mother passed away a few years ago and she knew that she would not live much longer because her illness was terminal, she suggested that his father should marry one of three of her best friends. This he did, and it worked out beautifully. And when he told me this, I proceeded to think seriously about the situation. When I decided to talk to this lady, my next question was would she say "yes." When I asked if she would allow me to visit her, she agreed that the two of us had lost our mates, and indirectly we found that we had some things in common.

It was quite interesting as to how we really started to seeing each other. When my wife died I decided to visit for a few days with my mother and one of my

127

sisters who lived together in St. Louis, Missouri. It's almost impossible to describe just how I felt after having lost my wife whom I had lived with for 32 years. I thought I wanted to return to my job immediately, and tried it, but it just didn't work. I fell out and tried to go from the office to the doctor's office, and a co-worker had to accompany me to the doctor where it was found that I had high blood pressure and was put on medication. This is when I decided to go for a visit with my mother and sister. I got a few things together and put out for Missouri early one morning, and when I got approximately fifteen miles on the way, my mind told me to check and see as to whether I had my medication. When I got out of the car and went to the trunk to check for my medicine, I found it was on the bumper of the car in my shaving kit. This, I thought was unbelievable that the kit would stay put for that distance without having fallen from the car. I drove approximately one hundred miles out of Louisville, Kentucky and found myself falling asleep, at least, three times. My mind told me it was time to go back home and wait for a better day.

Upon returning home my mind told me to invite the lady, in question, to go along with me on the trip and in case she would accept the offer it would serve a two-fold purpose. It would give each of us a chance to access the situation, and give Mother a chance to meet her as she had so beautifully encouraged me to get married again in case I wanted to. This lady had in mind to visit her family in Jefferson City, Tennessee, two or three days later, and when I invited her to accompany me to Missouri, I promised her that we would return early enough for her to make her trip on schedule. While in St. Louis, I thought it would be appropriate for us to visit with a sister-in-law in Jefferson City, Missouri, for a day. When she went on her trip to visit her family, she could tell them that she had been to Jefferson City, Missouri prior to the time she went home since it was less than two hundred miles from St. Louis. Instead of getting in touch with the sister-in-law to inform her of our proposed visit, we went to Jefferson City to find that she had been to Jefferson City, Missouri. The sum total of it all boiled down to the fact that I was trying to make an impression on the lady so that she might say "yes" when I asked her to marry me. In between, the times we saw each other prior to the time I popped the question to her were quite frequent. We visited her home some two or three times prior to our decision to get married; in fact, we decided to get married during a visit to her home. In fact we married at her parents' house. Quickly she called her children long distance to announce our decision and invite them to witness the occasion. In fact, her daughter asked her if she had to get married as it was a last minute decision. When we returned to Frankfort, she proceeded to move in with me, and it came as a surprise to many. And when I asked her where did she want to go on our honeymoon, she surprised me when she suggested going to the Smoky Mountains where she had lived most of her life, less than thirty miles away, but had never been to the Smoky Mountains.

This also reminds me when we decided to visit with relatives out in Oakland, California, in 1976. At our request, AAA routed us the most scenic way and the nearer way. We chose to go the most scenic way and return, the nearer way. We left Frankfort around seven o'clock on Saturday morning, and got less than seventy five miles from home to Mammoth Cave. She wanted to go through the cave, and mind you, it takes several hours to go through the cave. She has lived in Frankfort several years, and never thought about visiting the cave before, or since. We made no overnight reservations on the trip because we were not sure as to how far we would go each day as this was the most scenic way. We had studied the route in advance and were not sure as to how long we would tarry at certain points. For example, we were routed through or by-passed by Memphis, Tennessee. As this was within 69 miles from where we lived in Mississippi, when we moved to Missouri several years ago, I had not been back for twenty some years. So I suggested that we go to Jonestown.

I was so excited over the visit with those whom I had known through the years and had not seen for many years. Therefore, we overstayed our time, and when we left there we had to spend the first night in West Memphis, Arkansas. During the visit with friends in Mississippi, I visited with a couple whose husband taught school in Clarksdale, Mississippi. They took me to the school in that city where I attended for seven months, and I promised to pay him something like two or three dollars per week for transportation. Mind you, it was thirteen miles from Jonestown to Clarksdale, and when our parents decided to move to Southeast Missouri almost overnight, I left Mississippi owing this man for said transportation for three months which came out to the sum of approximately $33.00. I paid him at that time; I never before had a better feeling than at this time in all the days of my life because the man had helped me at a time when I needed it most, and it perhaps encouraged him to continue to help those in need of something that he had to offer. Last, but not least, it showed that I had made a few steps beyond working on the WPA for the family's livelihood and paid this debt after all of this time on my way to visit in California with relatives an friends.

There is a destiny that makes us brothers, none goes his way alone, all that we send into the lives of others comes back into our own.

We took our camera and took several pictures while on the trip, and my wife said when my time came to drive she would read what was expected to be seen of interest, along the way. But when her turn came to drive, I slept most of the time. On two occasions during the trip, we found ourselves driving a bit longer during the days and part of the night as a result of not having made advance reservations. At one point, we found ourselves staying at a motel that was undesirable, but again, we found that experience is the best teacher. As we approached the state line of California, we had to stop at a check point before entering the state of California where we were deprived of the items we had anticipated on taking with us such as fruits. When it was explained to us as to why they did this, we could understand why. They feared we would transport insects or disease or both from out of state. We arrived in Oakland, California at approximately 3:00 p.m., on Wednesday. And from then on through Saturday we were on the go. We visited in San Francisco while there, as it is located just across the bay from Oakland. We left Oakland early Sunday morning, around seven o'clock, en route for home. We came back the nearer route, and sometime, maybe around two hundred miles out of Oakland, the drive shaft went out on my car, a '72 LaSabre Buick. This being Sunday we wondered just what to do, but were fortunate in finding a garage, nearby, that put things together well enough for us to make it back home. And of course, I had to have a new drive shaft.

Thank goodness we were not ripped off on the trip. For example, when we went to Gainesville, Florida to visit with our son and his wife, on the way the air conditioner on my car ceased to function. We were forced to make a choice as to whether we would keep the windows closed in order to be able to

130

listen to the radio, or vice versa, and we decided to listen to the radio for a period and get a bit of air in between. I promised my wife that I would see that this would be corrected while in Florida, and enjoy both the radio and air on the way back home. We got within approximately one hundred miles from the state line of Florida, and the car stopped and we found that the alternator had gone bad. I at first thought that we were lucky to happen near a garage that we thought could help us. When they got through telling me what they found wrong with the car, it came to almost nine hundred dollars, and as we had more credit cards than cash, we found a bank that honored a card which my wife had. We got the money so that we could make the trip to Florida. My wife wanted me to replace the alternator and take a chance on getting to Florida without these other things that we were told was wrong, but it was five o'clock in the evening and I felt that this would be too much of a chance to take, especially at that time of day. We arrived at Gainesville, Florida after dark and had to find our way to the son's house. The next day I took the car to Sears Roebuck, as my credit was in good standing with them. When they completed the job on the air conditioner, it cost an additional six hundred plus dollars. At this point, I was reminded that the state troopers in Kentucky had told me that this kind of thing happens on highways. Now I can testify to this fact.

On our way back to Kentucky, we got approximately fifty miles over the state line into the state of Georgia, and I got a glimpse of smoke, from the rear, through the rear-view mirror. I asked my wife if it was coming from our car, and she said, "Yes." I immediately pulled over out of the traffic and raised the hood to find that the motor was on fire. Luckily there was a state trooper nearby who came over with his fire extinguisher and put the fire out before damage was done to the motor. He called for a wrecker, and I preferred AAA, but forgot to tell him until he had made the call. But the gentleman who responded to the call was very kind; when I told him about our misfortune while on the trip, he gave us a statement to AAA to that effect. They honored our request, and the mechanic only charged us for the hose which he installed plus his labor. This caused us to arrive home a day later than we had planned. We traveled extensively, more than twice the amount my late wife and I traveled during our thirty-two years together. In the first place, she did not drive, and secondly, she was not interested in

131

traveling, as I recall. At this time we only went to three states, Illinois, Missouri and Ohio. I love to travel, more so prior to the interstate highways. I must admit you get places faster, but you miss many interesting sights along the way.

Even in this modern age, I find people dying ahead of schedule because they don't know any better. Or some go to the doctor, and he tells them what they need, but for one reason or another they fail to take professional advice. I've heard many use such excuses as "That doctor doesn't know what he is talking about. The medicine is too expensive. I was suppose to go to the doctor today, but I feel alright. Therefore I am not going to keep the appointment. Or he never put his hand on me the last time and charged me thirty-five dollars." It is amazing to know the number of funerals we attend of people who diagnose their own cases and go to the drug store and purchase their own medications because, "The doctor is too expensive." Two years ago, the doctors (the reason I said doctors instead of doctor, is because I felt it necessary to get a second opinion) found that I had a blockage in my spine which prevented the blood from circulating properly in my spine. Not only for insurance purposes, but assurance purposes, I got a second opinion. The second doctor told me the same thing the first doctor told me, plus he said it was not unusual for this to happen to men my age. He further said that if you were my patient, I'd have you up walking the next day after the surgery. This was all I needed. This doctor was in Lexington, twenty-six miles away, and in case I chose him it would have been inconvenient for my wife and friends to visit me while in the hospital. Besides, my hometown surgeon who discovered this, had performed surgery on me before to remove a calcium deposit from my right shoulder, which was a success. Therefore, I chose him to do the surgery. I entered the hospital on the twenty-first day of September 1989 at which time he not only cleared the blockage, but purified my blood and restored it. When I was discharged from the hospital, October 5, 1989, they said I would need a walker, which I doubted. But I purchased the walker as a safety measure.

I was discharged on Tuesday, and took the walker home and used it the rest of the week. That was the end of the walker. The doctor told me to do anything I felt like doing, but just don't overdo it. This was during the fall when the leaves began to fall. I went out to rake a few leaves, and a neighbor was passing and saw what I was doing and stopped her car to ask if I wasn't overdoing myself. I agreed, and stopped, but I was used to doing it at that time of the year. Not only were the leaves falling, but with the beauty of the trees at that time of the year and the idea of what I had gone through successfully, I overdid it. I am a firm believer in my doctor and try to do whatever he says. Since that time I watched what I did and how I did what I did. The following spring I cut the grass once or twice per week, depending on how fast it grew, and walked from six to twelve miles on the track each week. Mind you, we have eleven thousand square feet of grass to cut.

Early in April 1990, the doctors found that I had cancer, three polyps on my colon that was cancer, and one was too close to my colon to be removed without removing a portion of the colon. One doctor told me that if I were his father, at my age, he would rather see me buried with my colon, than die on the operating table. My family physician was in the Persian Gulf with our armed forces during that war, and I felt compelled to do something immediately because cancer runs in our family. At age of seventy-nine, I was forced to do something as soon as possible. The thought came to me of our former physician, even though he was retired. I got on the phone and told him about my situation, and he advised that I should have surgery as soon as possible and even recommended the doctor to do the job. I immediately got in touch with the doctor recommended, and he made arrangements for me to go into the hospital April 8, 1990. The operation was scheduled for the 10th; on the 9th another doctor came in and examined me. Afterwards, he told me that all of my vital organs were OK, but my age was against me. I immediately told him what Shakespeare said about death,

Cowards die many times before their deaths, but the valiant never taste of death but once. Of all the wonders I yet have heard, it seems most strange that men should fear, seeing that death is a necessary end and will come when it will come.

At that moment I did take a second thought, knowing that I was seventy-nine years of age and I was scheduled for surgery the next morning at 7:30, and knowing that I was not put here to stay always. Therefore, I had many thoughts to run through my mind during the night. Most of all, I had a debt that I should tell my wife how to pay in case I didn't survive. Hoping she would arrive in time for me to discuss the situation with her, my room was located where I could see her when she arrived. Finally I saw her parking. At the same time, I heard personnel coming for me to go down for surgery, and I said, "Maybe I would live long enough to tell her, or suggest, just how to take care of two major bills that I owed." But with the wisdom of the doctors and nurses as well as the power of the medicine, and power from above, I was able to survive. I am a firm believer in doing what the doctors recommend.

The day before I was to have been discharged from the hospital, I made notes on certain things I wanted to discuss with the doctor prior to my departure for home. The last thing I jotted down was that I drink whiskey daily at home, and his reply to this was, "It won't hurt you; in fact, it might help you." He said that I should take daily exercise and not lift things that were heavy. I asked him just what he considered too heavy, and he said more than twenty-five pounds. I walk on the track from five to ten miles per week, including cutting our grass; and I haven't had any trouble since. And he also told me that I should check back with him within a year, unless I had problems before then. This was in April 1991, and during the early part of February, 1992 the news media constantly told how many people died the past year from colon cancer at a certain age, which included me, age-wise. So I began to have unusual feelings in the area of my stomach; therefore, I decided to check with him the first of March 1992, and he examined me to find that everything seemed OK. But he could tell that I was quite concerned because of the news media with regards to colon cancer, and decided to send me to the hospital for a complete physical which turned out OK. This made me feel that I was not having any trouble, so far as cancer concerned.

I remember one of the most exciting times of my early childhood was when one of my buddy's parents gave him a pocket watch for his birthday, a Waterberry, and I wanted one so bad I could hardly sleep at night. So my parents told me when I learned to tell the time they would give me one, and it didn't necessarily have to be on my birthday, whichever came first. Did I work hard on learning how to tell time! In fact, I believe I worked harder on this than any other project. And mind you, back in those days one didn't go to the jewelry store as today. It had to be ordered from a catalog, and it took two or three weeks to arrive when the order was made. And it seemed to me that it took two or three months for it to arrive. Not too many boys owned watches at that time, and when one owned a watch he stood out in the community, especially with the girls. Men were not wearing wrist watches during that time, and only a few women had watches. Today, instead of looking at my shadow, or listening to the train to determine the time of day, as I did on the farm of Mississippi, I have two watches, one pocket, to remind me of those bygone days, and the other wrist, that not only tells me the time of day, but the day of the week as well as the date of the month.

Men didn't own umbrellas at that time either; they wore the old fashioned rain coats (slickers), as they were called. Women used umbrellas during the summer as protection from the sun as well as during winter for rain. Not too many men owned house shoes, bath robes or pajamas. Mother made gowns, night gowns, as they were called; most men slept in their underwear. This may sound unbelievable, but we slept in this underwear each week. And mind you, we worked in this same underwear from Saturday till Saturday and dried on this same underwear when we took our Saturday night's bath. And during the summer, when we did certain jobs such as working hay, one sweated so freely that sweat ran down his pant legs into his shoes and sounded as though he had been wading in water. Nature had to be on our side at that time. Speaking of time, we had no time piece to carry to the field while we worked. In fact, we didn't need a time piece in the field, because we went to work as soon as daylight came, and could hear the train as it blew, around 10:30, as it passed through Darling, three miles away. In case we worked till twelve, we could always tell because one's shadow was cast close enough that he could step on his head shadow. And in many cases the plantation owners had huge bells mounted on a scaffold approximately twenty-five feet high with a rope or chain attached to the bell which extended within reach so that one could ring the bell four times daily, five or six days per week, depending on how much work to be done on the farm, usually between planting, cultivating and harvest time.

135

Animals, mules or horses or both, were used to cultivate the crops and were kept at a central location and were cared for by one or two men, depending on the size plantation. Those who lived on the plantation went to these men for working purposes as well as for the necessary tools to work with. These men were commonly known as, horslers; not only did they care for the animals, but did house work for the plantation owner. I knew very little about plantation living until early teenage, when we left the forty acre farm, on Squirrel Lake. I often wonder just why adversities come to one when he does his very best to serve his fellow man to the best of his ability as well as himself. But I also learned that the answer does not always come on your schedule; you must keep the faith and keep on keeping on.

My experience on the Mississippi plantations compelled me to get an education. I also learned that when we come to a certain point in life, we are forced to choose between life and death. Not literally. We must say goodbye to those whom we love best, even our parents. "Not that we love Caesar less, but we love Rome best." "Choose ye this day whom you will serve." At age twenty-five, with, not even a good high school education, I had to make this decision, and I attribute all this to my experience on the Mississippi plantation. "The evil that men do lives after them, but the good is often interred with their bones." I must admit, that I had to work like hell for what I've got, but I also learned that, "good things come to he who waiteth providing he worketh like hell while he waiteth." There may be some who question the statement about what I've got, but if they only knew where I came from, there would be no doubt about the statement about what I've got.

Many of those who form such opinions, of whom I know, should be independent at this point in their lives, at which time they need it most but are penniless. Their parents left property to them, debt free, and some don't even have the initiative to keep it up to par. Had it not been for the slum clearance, some of those same people would not have had a decent bathroom today. You might get one out of the slums, even though against your will, but you can't get the slums out of the individual. Many of those who were able to change their lifestyles as a result of the slum clearance, still have one or two old cars on their premises in need of repair and maybe on four flat tires. Still they become angry when the city forces them to either fix them or get rid of them. We have several pictures that were framed by one who worked for the state in this capacity for a meager wage and could have taken this work to his home that was left to him and his sister by their parents. He could have made more framing pictures on his own, at home, in one day than he got per month while working for the state. He could have not only owned his parent's home, but could have renovated it and lived comfortably for the rest of his life. But instead, he is renting, out of his meager retirement and going about town picking up tin cans to sell. This, plus other examples, have convinced me that we all would be surprised to know the percentage of any given local that has had many opportunities to have lived, and died independently. However, he had to be buried by the city in which they lived. This not only applies to those who did not go to school beyond their high school diploma, but those who went to college as well.

I used to rush home from school on Friday afternoons so that Mother could wash those trousers, that should have been dry cleaned, early enough so that I could press them in time to wear them on Sunday. They maybe had patches in the seat which caused me to wear a coat during the summer. Others of my age group were in their shirt sleeves. This not only hid the patches in my pants, but those in my shirt as well. We knew nothing about changing clothes with the change in season of the year, even though nature took care of the lower animals in this respect, that is, the texture of their bodies automatically changed with the changes of the seasons of the year. Their fur or hair protected them, but we wore the same clothing the year round, that is winter clothes because we could not afford both winter and summer wear.

But today we change with the seasons. When spring rolls around we not only put winter wear away, but do this in style, that is have them cleaned, or stored till the next season and bring out the summer wear. Instead of having one each for the change, I can change each, each seven days per week and still have some that I didn't get around to within a week's time. Instead of one pair of shoes only, and they sometimes needed repair which we could not afford, not even polish which cost only ten cents, but now I have between twenty-five and thirty pairs to choose from of various colors, and they cost enough for me to be justified in having them repaired when the need arises. Instead of the hair cut I used to get from a relative every once and awhile for ten cents, I go to the barber shop every two weeks and pay the customary price and leave at least a fifty-cent tip to the barber. I have at least one hundred and fifty neck ties to choose from when it comes to dressing. I used to change neck ties as the styles changed, that is when they switched from wide to narrow or just vice versa I'd go to the cedar chest and change accordingly. But here recently the styles changed to an in between, width wise, and the design changed; therefore, I was forced to restock all together. I could count my ties on one hand and 2 or 3 fingers And instead of going around toothless, as men sometime are prone to do when it comes to my age group, I have a two thirds partial of which one cannot tell, unless I tell them. I have dress shirts that I haven't worn within a years time, that is name brands. I have jackets that have not been worn over two or three times within a year's time.

At this point, I am again reminded of my first, secondhand radio, Crosley, which I purchased when I arrived in Frankfort, Kentucky during mid April 1937 for $12.50. My co-workers on the college farm could not understand the reason it upset me to no end when they turned on my radio without my permission. But when we lived on Squirrel Lake, in Mississippi, no one in the community had a radio, except a white family that lived approximately 1/2 mile away. We had permission to listen to certain programs, that we heard were to be aired at certain times, but we had to listen from the outside and had to walk from home to that point and back, after said program was over. This is, or was my reason for having been so particular about my radio. Only two or three others, out of thirteen of us on the farm had radios. We now have radios all over the house; in the master bedroom on either side of our bed, with telephones, on the night tables handmade from Pierce Furniture Company. And we have one in the living room which is portable, for convenience when one is outside on the lawn or patio. One is in the kitchen, and another one is in the den. I also shared my suits with one or two fellows who lived on the farm on special occasions and were around my size. I regret, many times that I failed to keep an ink blotter, from the post office where the Great Western Tailoring Company had sent to the local post office advertising my tailoring business.

I sometimes had mixed emotions while enjoying these modern facilities, because I felt that our parents would be proud to see me enjoying these facilities

138

after the struggle I went through the twenty-five years with my family. I always tried to keep Mother up to date with my progress after I left home because she was very supportive of my plans while I was with them.

When TV's came on the scene, I purchased my first one, black and white even before cables were available. We bought a seventy foot antenna, even though the programs were not very plain. But we enjoyed it along with others who did the same. Later, cables became available where not only were the programs better, but we had additional stations to select from. And when color was added, we purchased a set. When my parents found out, through a nephew who was enrolled at Kentucky State College, I was criticized by my mother who said that this was the reason I could not help them any more. I have no regrets for having stayed at home with my family twenty-five years, but from all indications they felt that I left too soon, including five sisters.

My nephew who finished high school with a pretty good record as a football player chose KY State to attend. We were proud of him, and he did well. He is still doing well as a coach out in Oklahoma. But during one of his visits home, he told somebody in the family that we had a colored TV, and I found later that this did not take very well with the family. For example, my late wife and I decided to go to Chicago on vacation to visit a friend for a week, but she did not feel comfortable without visiting my people who lived there at that time. I told her we'd visit the friend and make a pop call with my family while there. A day before our departure for home, I decided to give my relatives a ring. When they were told that we had been in Chicago almost a week without having gotten in touch with them, they thought it ridiculous for us not to have gotten in touch with them earlier. During the conversation we promised to spend the last night with them before returning home. Our friend understood the situation and agreed that we should go to them for the last night. We packed our bags and expressed appreciation for the pleasant visit and went to my sister's house. All five sisters lived in a complex which they purchased together. And in the meantime, Mother was there on vacation. When we arrived, we discovered that my baby sister's second child had a cast on one of his ankles that had practically worn off. I volunteered to take him to the hospital in order to get this corrected only to find that his mother owed the doctor five dollars which I paid. When we returned to the apartment, my wife was upset to no end and told me that they were criticizing me for having purchased a colored TV, instead of helping our parents. She demanded that we leave immediately and return to our friend's house for the last night. I tried to explain to Mother how unfair this was to us as much as I had sacrificed for the family through the years. Many things ran through my mind that I sacrificed myself for the benefit of my parents, sisters and brother. Further, I was now married to a woman whose parents had deceased, and I was her only means of support. Mother reminded me that I was her son which did not help the situation. She finally apologized to my wife who refused to accept her apologies. Our host was surprised when we returned so quickly, for she had taken sheets off the bed in which we slept, but without hesitation put them back on the bed for our last night in town. Most of our conversation on the way home was trying to convince her that she should accept Mother's apologies. Thank God she did. A few days after we returned home, she wrote Mother a nice letter stating that she had accepted her apologies.

On another occasion, Mother wanted me to buy a dress for Easter as a gift to her, but I answered her request in writing that I had recently purchased a bedroom suit for my wife. It cost only $103.00 and the mattress was thrown in without charges. This may sound cheap, which it would be today, but I was making only $7.00 a week as a bartender, and this I did in an effort to encourage my wife to accept her grandfather's offer to allow us to stay in his house without charges a while longer. But this didn't work with Mother either. When she received my letter of regrets, she passed it on to a sister who was teaching in another community, and she wrote me a letter stating that she was reading my letter to Mother at two o'clock in the morning. She expressed that they loved our Mother, but I didn't. This upset me to no end. And on another occasion mother became ill and required around the clock service, and I received a letter which stated how long Mother had been ill and how each of the five sisters had taken time out to take care of her and wanted to know when my wife would report for duty. After having discussed the situation with my wife, I suggested that we'd respond by finding out what the round trip between Frankfort, Ky., and Popular Bluff, Mo. would cost, and give them the choice as to which they'd rather. Of course, I would have been very disappointed had they chose her instead of the money, but after 25 years at home I had a pretty good idea that they would accept the money.

At one time I lost quite a bit of sleep over these types of things, but not anymore. Even though I had to work like a slave to get what I have, I got it. Everything did not come on my schedule, but it came in due time, and we enjoyed life to the fullest extent. My former co-workers, in state government, always said that I could find a parking place in the parking lot when no one else could, at anytime of day.

I just recently received my twenty-year pin for having volunteered with the Red Cross from the day I retired and still do. The very best things in life are living it. And I worked for a living, and retired to live. I've also learned that it's not the amount of money that one makes that counts, but it's how you use it. I've known many people, right here in Frankfort, who had all kinds of opportunities to have retired decently, but unfortunately, due to mismanagement they are penniless and depending on Red Cross for their livelihood. Those who bet on the race horses and play the lottery cannot afford it and seldom win.

I sometimes wonder if I had joined the native Frankfortonians instead of what I did in the way of struggling in an effort to become a decent tax payer as a property owner would my late wife have survived, or would I have succeeded her in death? She told me many times that in case I died first she wondered how would she handle the mortgage. It was only one hundred and fifteen dollars per month, for twenty years, and I told her each time she brought the subject up, that she could find somebody in need of a place to live to come in and share the expense as well as be company for each other. And in case one didn't work out, just keep trying, surely there is somebody in the community that would be compatible. The house could easily be converted into two apartments with an entrance in the basement already accessible from the outside. The community consists of quite a few widows whose husbands have deceased since we built the house.

The majority of our inhabitants either built or purchased houses that were built for sale by the realtor, around the same time. One neighbor told me, during the time his house was being built that he would not be able to live long enough to see that his house was paid for, but he planned to enjoy it as long as he lived. And his widow, along with others who had similar experiences are doing well. But it just kept running through my mind that the majority of those referred to were not Frankfortonians and are still going along with their lives. Even though they are lonely and out of this number, I haven't seen one as yet who had to share their homes with someone else in order to pay for them. And I've been here, in this house, many years. The community is ideally located on the hill, overlooking the city and there is only one way in and out, which means that those who come in must go out the same way which they came in. The only problem that some have to deal with is living next door to houses that were built for sale, not as demonstrators, but by realtors that just built for sale, and therefore, were not well built. In fact, one or two had to be redone before they could be sold, and this is where one, unfortunately, might have problems to deal with.

But when one looks around at other new subdivisions that were being built at the same time we built, our problems are not so bad after all. Incidentally, most of our problems come from those who purchased those houses that were referred to above. For example, there are those who, maybe only one in the household, have two cars and others with three or four cars, a truck and until recently owned a boat of which has not been in the water for years. And the truck, he doesn't need because he is supposed to be a teacher at the University. There are two Pontiacs, a Cadillac and a Chevrolet; his wife drives one of the Pontiacs, as she teaches in another town, approximately 25 miles away. His daughter, who is presently enrolled at the local university, drives the Chevrolet, and he alternates with his transportation between the other Pontiac, the Cadillac and the Ford truck. Their next door neighbor, who is also a school teacher, owns two nice Buicks but drives only one. One day I asked her why not sell one, as its value is decreasing by the day. Her answer was, "I keep it in memory of my husband." He purchased each of these automobiles, plus a Buick, and only he and the wife drove. In fact, they were the only people in the household at that time. I was in school with these two people and envied each of them, because in the first place I was twelve or fifteen years older than they. Also, she ran for Miss Kentucky State during our time in college, and he qualified for the pros in football, and did play professional football for a while. For some reason he decided to return to the classroom as a physical education teacher and coached football. But he changed schools, quite frequently in and out of the state, these same people came to me seeking a place to rent when I purchased our first house, which had two apartments but was already rented.

This caused me to look back at our college years when I envied them. Even our English teacher ignored me during class discussions, and I attributed this to my age, and the fact that no one knew whence I came, and could care less. And in later years, when I finished college and my accomplishments were beyond theirs, as a tax paying citizen and property owner, the English teacher remained at the College long enough, in fact until she retired, to see the difference in the older student who came out of nowhere and was not known by those in the community. Therefore, I gained respect after all of these years and was told, indirectly, by said instructors at the College they gained respect for me by the progress I made as a *public spirited citizen in the community.*

It took me all of these years to get the answer as to why I decided to "cast down my bucket" here in Frankfort after graduation. I am now reminded of the teacher whom I went to, to approve a subject I needed to meet the requirement for graduation in my field, vocational agriculture, which he taught. I admired him very much because he was a member of the fraternity that I had a high regard for, and had planned to join, if accepted. And the latter two words impressed me most, because at this time in my life one should be very cautious as to the direction he decides to go, and I had heard that this professor had recently met the requirements for his Ph.D. degree. Yet upon entering his office I congratulated him and this was an insult to him. He told me that he had no Ph.D., and if I was not fully prepared to meet the requirements in his class, I had better go some place else. It upset me to no end; I took the subject, and passed it, and after graduation I worked up in state government, first as a child welfare worker, Assistant Supervisor of Adoptions, and finally Chief Employment Counselor. Somewhere down the line, I was invited to this professor's class to talk on my work. During the introduction, I was so flabbergasted I hardly knew just what to say or where to start on whatever I had to say. I have found, even in this late day of my life, that regardless the grade which one might obtain in the classroom, or the degree he might obtain from the university, wherever it might be, he still might not be educated as *per se*.

It matters not where you were born or when you were born, but it's what's born when you were born.

During the past twenty years I became dissatisfied with the church which I belonged to, which happened to be Baptist operated. Ever so often I am reminded of the statement which was made to me in Okolona Industrial Junior College, in Okolona, Mississippi by one of the English professors. It took me fifty years to realize just what he meant when he said that I was "too intelligent" to be in the Baptist church. The nearer Sunday morning came, the more I became dissatisfied; therefore, fourteen years ago I joined the First Christian Church, (Disciples of Christ). Prior to the time I joined the church, I visited many other churches, all Baptist, except the one which I joined, but none appealed to me like the First Christian. I'm on my fourth, three-year period as a deacon. During my second term I was captain of my communion team which consisted of seven elders and twenty-five deacons. We were responsible for the communion, each Sunday, during the months of September-December, March and June. Dr. Carl Smith is Director of the Music Department. At that time, he and I were the only black members of the church. This church consists of members from all walks of life; and each member plays leading roles in the church. We work by a schedule; that is, we start on time and end on time. We are out of our morning service in time to go to any black church in time for the sermon. We broadcast on the radio each Sunday, but one can stand on the outside of the church and hear the sermon at the black church, in most cases. Obsequies at our church go from twenty to thirty minutes, but in most cases, twenty minutes is the limit. But in black churches it goes on and on. I can see why black kids lose interest in the church when they return home from college where everything is done on schedule. I can also see why programs, in the black churches, are operated as such because the professional members take the back seat and use less voice in the church. Therefore the church program is failing; black kids are sent to church instead of being accompanied by their parents. This is also true in the extra curricular programs. We live within a block of the athletic field where such games as

144

football, baseball, soccer and track meets are held, in their seasons each year. But they are almost segregated in the opposite direction; that is, one can almost count the black participants on one hand. Where are they? On the street corners, at home, in bed -- no jobs, no future. I often wonder where do, or how do the census personnel get their figures on the unemployed, when fast food places have signs out which indicate, "We are hiring."

I believe the homes and churches are neglecting their responsibilities; and the poor school teachers are underpaid and have very little, if any, voice when it comes to disciplining the kids. This may be responsible for many of those who would be dedicated teachers seeking employment in industries. A few years ago, I spoke with a patient, as a Baptist and he was a Methodist, and since deceased. We discussed this subject in the hearing of his late daughter's mother-in-law who is also Baptist; and I noticed that she was quite silent during the conversation. I didn't pay any attention to that until a few days later at which time I received a letter from her indicating that she did not appreciate what I said at the hospital about her pastor, who was mine also at that time. She further stated that prior to that time I had always been "Mr. Simmons" to her, but from that day forward I was "just plain" George Simmons. I admire the lady, even though later years, having come into the church and playing a leading role, sings in the choir, etc. But *"ye shall know the truth and the truth shall set you free."* I played a leading role in the selection of this minister for our church. At that time I was Assistant Superintendent of the Sunday School, and was thrilled to no end when he accepted the call in November 1960. The reason I remember this so well I was attending the University of Louisville, School of Social Work.

This was also the time of the great debate between the late President John Fitzgerald Kennedy, and Richard M. Nixon. I watched in my room on the campus, and Mr. Kennedy won. I was thrilled over the fact that Mr. Kennedy won the debate, as well as we won the minister of our choice to become the pastor of our church at the same time. I said he is young, and I'm sure he is going to bring us up-to-date trends in our church program. Upon his arrival, we noticed that he was not fully equipped in his attire, so far as changing clothes with the change of the season. It was obvious when he came out in a raincoat whether it was rain, or sleet, or snow. After a period, I took it on myself to discuss this with a few

145

members of the church, and with their permission, I solicited money from members of the church to purchase him an overcoat. I was happy to report the response which I received. After having collected a certain amount, which I regret that I am not prepared to report, I invited the minister to accompany me to Lexington, to Graves Cox, the leading men's store in this area. At that time, and upon arrival at the store, I suggested that he select an overcoat of his choice, and he did. Afterwards, I found that there was money left, and I suggested that he select from other items, which I don't remember his choice. But at the end, I found that there was still money left; therefore, I gave him the remainder. This thrilled me to no end because I felt that this was a new, young man, with up-to-date ideas, and we were about to go places. I could see us having something in common and would gain more strength and knowledge about the Bible.

But things did not work out the way I thought they would; in the first place, the man didn't have any respect for time. I wouldn't be surprised if the man would be late for his own funeral, if he had anything to do with it. Not only was time a problem but values as well; the church was built in 1908 by those who made sacrifices in order to construct the edifice, church, annex and garage. I understand that they had quite a battle in court in order to get the location on which to build. But they won the battle with good legal backing, thank God. Looking at the situation at this point, those who were responsible for the buildings and ground would be quite unhappy to see how it is being treated today. The parsonage, church, annex and garage are all falling apart. The concrete steps need rails, especially for the older citizens. The buildings haven't had a decent paint job for years; if something isn't done soon, I'm afraid that the city will be forced to condemn certain parts of the plot. Maybe the quicker this happens the better it will be, because after a point it will be beyond repair. On one occasion, my wife and I attended a wake at the church, and she discovered that she was sitting on a nail head. As she moved over, a member of the church discovered what had happened, and called it to the pastor's attention. He immediately got a hammer and came over and drove the nail down while others watched and apparently didn't think anything about it. There have been occasions when a member passed away while he was out of town. Regardless of where he was, or the occasion, if he came to preach the funeral, he charged the family a fee. I think this is ridiculous. This is a part of my reason for leaving the church. The majority rules, and I was in the minority; therefore, I felt that it was time to move out.

I feel much more comfortable after I moved my membership. A few friends questioned my move from the Baptist faith; in fact, I really wanted to consider one of the local Baptist churches, but I had mixed feelings about some of their expressed opinions about black people. In fact, the then pastor of that church almost won me, but I followed my mind and was very glad that I did. He did not remain there too much longer after I made my decision to move as I did. Dr. Carl Smith, head of the music department, had much influence over my option to make the move to the Christian Church. Not only is he an excellent music director, but he also brings along students from Kentucky State University, on special occasions to participate in the church programs.

We, as human beings, sometimes jump to conclusions too quickly. For example, I was in the church Sunday School class almost a year before having been asked to play an individual part in the Sunday School program. And the very first time I was asked to participate was on Saturday. The president of our class met me at a local service station where we both got gas, and he asked me if I would have the prayer during the devotion on Sunday morning. I gladly gave my consent, but had not looked at the subject to be discussed. Immediately, when I got home I decided to familiarize myself with the subject. And low and behold, the subject was on "slavery." This caused me to have mixed emotions, being the only black member of a class of approximately twenty-five. And when time came for the invocation, I thanked God for having broken down the walls of partition between slaves and free men, Greeks and Barbarians, Jews and Gentiles, the North and the South, the East and the West.

Shame our jealousy and lay low our pride, break down, we beseech thee, the wall that divides us one from another.

When the devotion ended, I wondered if I shouldn't continue in prayer by not having opened my eyes, or just what next, but the response was just the opposite; everyone seemed to have enjoyed it.

147

Not only have I been president of the class on two different occasions, but I am presently vice president. In fact, the entire congregation seems to consider me as just another member of the church family, for which I'm grateful. I have reservations as to what my dad would think about my change in my religious faith, as he was a Baptist minister. During my search for a church home, I had in mind to remain in the Baptist church. But I have a feeling that Mother would go along with me because she had become dissatisfied with the way Black Baptist churches operated during the latter part of her life. In fact, she told me after she returned home after having visited with us on one occasion, that she wrote my then Baptist pastor a letter which he never answered. I could imagine why he, maybe, did not respond because she and I thought alike when it came to the way we as a race conduct our religious services.

But I knew of some, maybe I should say one in particular, who demonstrated his feelings about the subject when we, as a race, were demonstrating in the form of sit-ins, asking for admittance to the public facilities, to be treated as a human, not special, but just as everyone else was treated. No one was asking for a hand-out; of course we all know about those of every race, color, or creed who go around looking for something for nothing. During the mid-sixty's, my late wife and I decided to join the students from Kentucky State College after the morning service at our church, during a march around Frish's Big Boy, in an effort to get permission to be admitted for lunch and be served, like everyone else. As we marched around the restaurant, single, approximately five feet apart, there was an individual on the entrance door to allow whites in between the marchers. In case a black attempted to enter the door behind a white person, he closed the door in his or her face. *And believe it or not, the doorkeeper was the deacon of the church I would have considered to transfer my membership to!* Not only was he a deacon of the church, but he taught the Sunday School lessons over the radio each Sunday. My late wife frequently told me how she enjoyed his teachings on the radio; in fact, he might have caused her to refuse to join me in going to Sunday School during our marriage. This experience surprised me to no end. In fact, when we arrived home after the demonstration, I called his home and his wife answered the phone. She told me that he was not home at the time, but she would have him to return my call. He did, and I told him how much he disappointed us at the restaurant that day with regards to his refusal to admit us into the facility, and how my wife had enjoyed his Sunday School lessons over the radio each Sunday, and that I feared she would not listen to him from that day forward. She said she would have him to return my call. He did, and I told him how much he disappointed us at the restaurant that day with regards to his refusal to admit us into the facility, and how my wife had enjoyed his Sunday School lessons over the radio each Sunday, and that I feared she would not listen to him from that day forward or she would not feel the same. Even if she listened, it would not be as meaningful as before. I also reminded him of not only his influence in the community, but with this and the share which he had in the restaurant, this could become a reality overnight. The conversation came to a halt when he hung up on me, and this changed my thoughts when it came to considering his church as a choice to join.

But I find that the church is no different from other community organizations. They are all operated by people; regardless of the denomination or faith, we should take the Bible for our guide and become familiar with its teachings and observe them; seek wisdom and prosperity from our Heavenly Father. As we grow in stature, in bodily strength, and in years, we should assume more of our responsibility toward our fellow man; let us aspire to be men and women of the noblest character, and cherish the feelings that we were born with, not only to receive good, but to do good.

One of the most difficult decisions I had to face was to retire at age sixty-two, three years short of being eligible for social security. I suffer from a sinus condition, and at that time it had reached the stage where I was forced to resort to medication in order to get relief. As a result of the polluted or morally corrupt in state government, the nearer Monday morning came the worse I felt. And when I resorted to medication for relief, which made me groggy, many times I found myself falling asleep during the times I should have been at work. But at that time, I had applied for one of two positions that became vacant as a result of one who retired at that time. In fact, I received a letter, from the personnel department which suggested that I should do so in case I was interested. In the meantime, many of my white friends who were in higher positions encouraged me to make application for one of the positions. They knew the job descriptions compared with my qualifications for either of the two jobs. Only one out of four whom I talked with in regards to the two positions told me that I would qualify. And when I told one of those who encouraged me to make application what this individual said, he told me to disregard him because I not only qualified for these jobs, but for the job which this fellow held. After having submitted my resume, as was requested from the personnel office, I was told that there were others who had applied also for this particular job. Being the only black in line for the job, I decided to discuss the situation with one of my black brothers who was in charge of the Equal Opportunity Office. He should have and could have executed his duties of that office to see that I was considered for the job. But during my discussion with him in this regard, he had me to know that the man had already been selected for the job on his ability to tell dirty jokes. I invited him to step outside of his office and take a look at the sign over his door which read, "Office of Equal Opportunity in Employment." This gave me the answer as to why I was not considered for the job which he held because they wanted a "yes man."

All of those who were in power at that time knew that I would not fit into the situation because they knew me from the days of my janitorial service in that agency. For example, during my tenure as a janitor in the year 1949, some of the office equipment disappeared from time to time. Eventually, the fellow who was responsible for what was going on was finally caught and fired, and in the meantime I was told that I knew what was going on but refused to report the situation, and in case such should occur again (and I knew it and failed to report it), I would be kicked in my pants. I told him that that would be the last time he would kick anybody with that foot because he would be minus a foot.

I am also aware of the fact that we who strive for top positions in employment are faced with as much opposition on one side of the railroad track, as the other. Had this man who was in the position of Equal Employment Representative made it known to the proper source that this job was given to the man who told the best jokes, chances are he would not have gotten the job. Neither would I or any other Black have been considered for the job on this basis.

150

In 1970, a student after having graduated from Kentucky State came to the Department of Economic Security as an employee. Immediately he became the personnel director's right hand man. At the same time he moved into our community, not only on the job, but at social events. I recall on one occasion they appeared at a basketball game, and the gym was crowded. But I saw one seat which was vacant and pointed it out to him. He refused to take it because he refused to leave his crony. And I thought at that time I should as a neighbor and one who had been acquainted with the politicians some twenty odd years, tell him what the score was with his running mate. So the very next time I got a chance to talk with him was in the restroom at work. I told him that I had observed him to have been closely allied with the Director of the Personnel. I was aware that he would one day sooner or later be fired because of his unbecoming conduct in that office. I also reminded him of the fact that he and I were from the Deep South, he from Alabama and I from Mississippi. But I had been allied with the political machine long enough to know what goes on. And, mind you, he too was black and was fully aware of how we were both treated in our respective states when it came to the race issue and job opportunities. He was eager and anxious to be considered for a promotion on his job, and I was striving for a better job or promotion so that I could, within the next three years retire. In that time would have been perfect so far as social security was concerned. Three days later, I was never before so embarrassed as when three co-workers who were white and I were on our way to the cafeteria on break and met the Personnel Director on the way. He told the fellows that they perhaps didn't know it, but they were running with a no good fellow. "George Simmons, is no good." This reminded me of the story about crayfish in a barrel. When one starts climbing the side of the barrel, before he reaches the top in order to free himself, the one just below reaches up and pulls him back.

I've held many jobs over the past twenty years of my retirement. During the first four years, I worked with the Revenue Department seasonally, five months each year during income tax filing time, but I hardly knew what to do with myself during the remaining seven months. I was very fortunate in obtaining a job with the Habilitation Center. I enjoyed it very much, for three reasons. First, it enabled me to use the experience which I obtained as a handicapped specialist during my

151

tenure in state government, since this job dealt with the handicapped in training them for employment. Many were trained and placed in permanent employment after a period of on the job training. Secondly, I was employed twelve months during the year. And thirdly, the pay was good. But unfortunately I was able to stay in this job only one year because my retirement benefits were too good, according to the Senior Citizen Center, where I visited those in the hospital and homebound, delivered lunches, and drove the bus for one year. But one thing I could not understand was that I took a black patient to a black doctor who refused to treat him because he owed him twenty-five or thirty dollars. I took him to the hospital where he was given proper treatment, and this same doctor was my family doctor. He frequently issued sample medications to patients and charged them for the same. White doctors issued the same to their patients and without charge. During my two years and four months with this agency I became somewhat dissatisfied because of the same reason I left the Revenue Department. The schedule was only one-half day, five days per week.

During this time, the Capital Plaza Hotel was erected here in Frankfort. I decided to make application for a job with the hotel. Not too long after I submitted my application, I was called in for an interview, which was quite favorable. They wanted me to be SSI representative for the hotel, but again it was found that my retirement benefits disqualified me for the job. Then we talked in terms of a position as Captain of the Bellboys, which I gladly accepted. There were three whites and one black on my staff. It was right interesting, when one of the whites found out what the setup was like, he came to me and asked, was he to work for me or with me. I immediately told him that he was to work *with* me. The setup worked out harmoniously.

The three whites were local fellows, but the black being from New York (just very recently established himself in the community) was not fully clad. For example, he had no black shoes which all bellmen were to wear, and he could not afford to purchase a new pair of shoes at that time. I suggested that he dye his brown shoes black which he agreed to, but he did not have the money for which to purchase the dye. He asked me to loan him five dollars in order to purchase the dye. A ten dollar bill was the smallest bill I had at that time, so he suggested that he could pay back ten dollars as easy as five. I went along with his suggestion, and two pay days came and I did not hear from him. So I asked for my money, and he said that he had to pay his rent. So I put pressure on him and demanded my money, so he responded. I always watched the big city boys because they seem to think they can get by on Southerners. Not too long after this event, he gave up his job. But as a whole, the fellows were very cooperative.

During my tenure as Bell Captain at the hotel, the owner of the facility decided to run for Governor of the Commonwealth of Kentucky. I supported him one hundred percent. But I still felt that the Lieutenant Governor would have made a better Governor, and I told him, the Lieutenant Governor, that I felt that way. He seemed to have understood; I sent out over three hundred letters to friends and relatives on his behalf. During this time I met the Honorable Harold Washington, Mayor of Chicago, Illinois, while attending my granddaughter's high school graduation. During our conversation, I found that he was a native of Winchester, Kentucky, and I immediately solicited his support for Mr. Wilkinson, as he had roots not only in Winchester but in other parts of the state.

I shall never forget an experience which I had during my tenure as a member of the Selective Service System (Draft Board), in 1974. There was a written standard by which men were supposed to be called into the service, but on one occasion they (the rest of the Board members which were all white, but me) decided to deviate from the law between two white draftees by delaying the one for a few days until he became 26 years of age which would automatically exempt him from the draft at that time. He was from a permanent family in the community, well liked, but was not gainfully employed. The other one was the son of the Human Rights Commissioner for the Commonwealth of Kentucky, and was in another state at that time in law school as a student. According to the law, the first one should have been drafted first, but the Board was determined not to draft him first because of his father's position. For the same reason I was determined to report the situation to the Adjutant General. After a series of conferences with concerned citizens with regards to the situation, it was decided that we should draft the one first. I find that prejudice is like a double bladed ax; it not only cuts on both sides, but is used by the power-to-be, on both sides of the railroad track when it comes to promotions in employment.

During my tenure in state government over the years, I find that there is as much or more prejudice among white folks as there is among blacks. I am the third black to run for City Commissioner in this community, and the first to win the primary election. The first two individuals were native Frankfortonians. I obtained nearly 2,000 votes in the race for the Office of City Commissioner although this was 2,000 votes short of a seat on the Commission. This should indicate something specifically about the political progress of Frankfort's black community. What does it indicate in terms of the political involvement of Kentucky State University's predominantly black student body, faculty and staff?

Approximately 1,500 blacks in Frankfort were registered voters at that time, and they represented particularly two voting precincts, Hickory Hill and Fairview. I carried both but faired better in Hickory Hill. I may not be remembered as the first real contender to be a city official, but the example I demonstrated could be an indicator for the future, especially the future political prospects for the city's black community.

As a result of my effort, I suggested that the black community here groom its own candidates to be spokesman and representatives, in advance, collectively. That we did in the last City Commission race, and as a result our black candidate, not only won, but led the field in that race. As a result, he is Mayor pro-tem. During my race for a seat on the City Commission, the political involvement of Kentucky State University students was virtually non-existent. With almost 1,400 black students, 1,150 of them old enough to vote, Kentucky State University might determine the outcome of many elections and referendums. However, it is evident the political participation in civic affairs by the University is negligible, and thus the entire political process here is cheated. The competition for University voters has yet to be born. I committed myself to challenge the traditional political elements of our city. I welcomed the challenge, and struggled through the primary and general election. I did not win, but perhaps my efforts might have motivated the politically-oriented black citizens to support the last black candidate who is presently Mayor pro-tem. As a result, I feel that he reaped some benefits from my labor, after having won the primary without the support from students from the University.

While campaigning on the campus prior to the primary, I saw some three or four plaques displayed on the front door of the Chapel between the metal bar and the glass of others who were running for election. Some were running for the same office I ran for. But mine, which was displayed first, was not to be seen because it was covered by those who liked the idea and did likewise with their plaques. Even though I pulled mine from behind and placed it where it could be seen, I knew I did not have the support from the campus because they should have corrected this instead of me. It was a mistake in allowing this to happen, and it was obvious that it was no question as to the racial identity because I was the only black in the race. Even though it could be said that they did not know me, I live just across the highway from the Campus and graduated from the University. I have been an active member of the local chapter of the Alumni Association since the day I graduated. It could not be said truly that I was an "Uncle Tom," and if they had any questions with this regard, I was never questioned even though I talked with students, collectively as well as individually, regarding the issues and this was never mentioned.

In my opinion what we do for others is not always returned from them or those whom we do the favors for. As a poet has so beautifully said,

There is a destiny that makes us brothers, none goes his way alone, all that we send into the lives of others comes back into our own.

I believe with all my heart, that there are but a few days, if any, pass but what I don't receive benefits from something that I've done for others in the past. Two or three years ago I lost my billfold at a homecoming game at Kentucky State University just as we, my wife and I, along with another couple, entered the football stadium. I decided to purchase a program. While making the change I missed my overcoat pocket, dropped my billfold, and did not realize I had dropped it until I was about ten feet from the ticket window. I immediately turned back and asked those who stood by if they saw me drop my billfold, and the answer was "No." I immediately joined my wife and guest at our designated seats, and when I told them the story, my wife asked if anyone had reported it to the press. Of course the answer no because I had no idea that anybody would return a billfold with twenty dollar bills and four or five credit cards. But I decided to follow through by reporting it to the press for whatever it was worth. As I approached the guard on duty at the press entrance, I asked her if I could report a lost billfold and she asked if it had my name in it. I told her no, but my initials were in it. She asked what was my initials were, and I told her "GWS." She pulled the billfold out of her pocket and gave it to me. I was afraid to open it, because I knew it would be empty. But finally I got up enough courage to open it, and found everything was there just as before. I then asked her who brought it to her, and she replied, "Two boys, apparently approaching early teens." I looked at my ticket and asked her, if possible, to direct those boys to my seat. Fifteen or twenty minutes later here come two boys who sat beside me, but said nothing. A minute or two it came to me that these are the boys who found my billfold, and I asked them if they were the ones. One replied, "Yes sir, me and him." He pointed to his companion, and I gave them a twenty dollar bill, told them to divide it, and said how nice I thought it was for them to demonstrate their honesty. They thanked me, and ran away. I then turned to those spectators nearby and asked them if they thought I gave the boys enough. Their response was yes. Those boys not only saved me $80 dollars in cash, but two or three credit cards and the billfold as well as many sleepless hours.

The following Monday, I went to the Senior Citizens Center, as I often visit, to find they had a surplus of approximately one hundred loaves of bread that were given to the Center by the Kroger store. They usually do so when such items are not sold by a certain time. I loaded the bread in the trunk of my car and began to distribute it to those senior citizens whom I knew would appreciate it. I knew from past experience as I had worked with the senior citizens two years and four months some four or five years ago. And the very first house where I started with the delivery, I opened the trunk and told the lady to get whatever she needed. She took only two loaves, and as she left she told me how glad she was to learn that I found my billfold. I asked her how she knew about me losing my billfold, and she said that her grandson was one of the two boys who found it. I told her that I gave them ten dollars each and wondered if that was enough. She said the child was tickled and ran home to tell her about it and asked her if he could buy a pizza with his ten dollars. This made me very happy because she told me the same as

156

others, that they were well-pleased with what I gave them. I immediately went to The State Journal to publish the honesty in the boys, where I was advised not to mention them by name because some of their peer group would probably belittle them for having turned the money in, instead of having kept it.

It's difficult, sometimes, to be honest, especially when one is in dire need. For example when I first came to the farm where I worked for seven dollars and fifty cents per month for my education, I had a chance to take an expensive pocket watch from a drunken man who wandered over to our quarters. In fact, I did take the watch from the man, and he staggered on his way from the farm. But before he got too far from the farmhouse, my mind told me to catch him and give him his watch. That I did, and I never was so relieved before. Had I kept this man's watch and the college authorities found that I did it later, chances are I would have been put out of school to never return again. I was again reminded of the plow which I attempted to take in Mississippi and narrowly escaped being caught. Even though hard, sometimes it seems impossible to resist temptation, especially when one has tried every imaginative way to do right. This reminds me of a statement by a the French novelist Colette (1873 - 1954) which I read sometime ago:

Look for a long time at what pleases you, and for a longer time at what pains you.

❖

One of my college professors always told his classes that one of the first things to do when you decide to establish yourself in the community is go to the bank and borrow money and pay it back on time. I adopted this motto during my last two years in college and have borrowed money from the bank on many occasions and have never been refused. In fact, I made a big mistake when I decided to retire, December 31, 1974 and lacked three and one-half years of being eligible for full benefits. But with three and one-half years of military service, I had a choice, but to purchase my military service which made me eligible to retire from

157

State Government with full benefits. The military service cost two thousand seven hundred and fifty dollars. I had the cash instead of borrowing this amount from the bank. I took it out of my savings and never did replace it; whereas, had I borrowed this amount from the bank and paid it back on the monthly installment plan, I would have retained the cash which I never did replace. It seems easier to pay on a loan than to pay one's self.

It pays not to act during a passion of anger or irritation. I was quite disturbed over the polluted politics; the job or position was not always given to the person who was best qualified to do the job, but in many cases to him who best satisfied the giver of the position. Had I taken a second thought with regards to my personal benefits, I would have continued in my job for three more years in order to qualify with full benefits from the Social Security Agency. I still have reservations about this situation, because I might have earned more money during my retirement period, up to the present. But I had the priceless privilege of many new contacts I made during this time. As I have often said, had I not retired at that time, I might not have lived as long as I have, and I'm sure I could not be any happier. So many times I've thought about a statement made by the former Vice President Hubert H. Humphrey (1911-1978), *"To err is human. To blame someone else, is politics."* I recall countless numbers of those whom I've known who retired and went home and sat in their favorite chair and within six months they had passed away.

❖

According to *Funk and Wagnalls Student Standard Dictionary* --

"Time is the portion allotted to human life or to any particular life, or purpose."

Time and how one handles it are essential.

Times could be hard for a small boy growing up on Squirrel Lake, three miles from Darling, Mississippi, especially at the Simmons' household where a father was out attending church conventions or revivals, and mother and I were at home trying to make ends meet for five sisters and one brother, all younger than I, craving life's simple pleasures like a decent pair of dress shoes, a suit of clothes, and cash in the pocket. Many times I've gotten change for a nickel, dime, or even a quarter to jangle in my pocket to give an impression that I had some money. During my late teenage years I worked on many jobs, for pay, by the day, such as cutting cordwood or working at the gin stand, but I never saw my paycheck because Dad always remembered when payday rolled around and was always on time to pick up my check. He spent it for the family needs. I always had to be the workhorse in the family. Once a workhorse, always a workhorse. This is why I felt comfortable on many of the jobs I held during my college years and beyond my college years. Often I've been asked why I know so many people, and the answer is, I either worked with them or for them, or both at sometime or another.

There is a destiny that makes us brothers, none goes his way alone,
all that we send into the lives of others comes back into our own.
(Author Unknown.)

The older I become, the more I understand the old saying that *"the rougher the road the sweeter is the journey at the other end."* Thank God through it all that I honored my parents to the best of my ability. As a result, everything I've attempted, almost, has been a success. Those things that I considered a failure, I didn't need in the first place.

159

PROFESSIONAL TRIBUTES

Chapter 4

Be not an idle dreamer.
Someday the Lord will call.
Call for the gift he gave us,
And we must account for all.

No calling is disgraceful,
But the disgrace consists of
Not performing well the
Duties assigned us.

(Author Unknown)

PROFESSIONAL TRIBUTES

Chapter 4

Many times when I'm in the den while reading the newspaper, watching TV, dwelling upon past times at the hotel or other jobs, reminiscing, or just sitting and doing nothing, I can't help but glance at a letter or two, among many, which I have on the wall. I shall attempt to share a few of these letters with you at this time. This is what I mean when I say that minimum wages are healthy if they are accepted with the right attitude. Minimum wage jobs give an employee the chance to prove his worth.

James L. Peel
1260 Meadow Lane
Frankfort, Kentucky 40601-4574
May 22, 1993

Mr. Kelly Hubbard, Chairman
Nominations Committee
207 College Heights
Hodgenville, Kentucky 42748

Dear Kelly:

I would like to recommend Mr. George W. Simmons Jr. for consideration
for both the Waterfield Achievement Award and the Waterfield Humanitarian
Award for 1993.

Mr. Simmons was born in the Mississippi Delta Region, one of several
children born to an itinerant Baptist Minister. He grew up amid the grinding
poverty and rigid segregation which typified that day in the rural South and
discouraged the advancement of Afro Americans. Despite these formidable
obstacles, Mr. Simmons managed to complete grade school in Mississippi and
later graduated from a segregated high school in Missouri where his father's
ministry had taken the family. After being graduated, Mr. Simmons took an
examination which qualified him to teach grade school. By agreeing to live in a
less-than-desirable area, he secured a teaching assignment which paid $30 a
month. By living hand-to-mouth, he was able to contribute to his family's support
and to the education of his brothers and sisters.

Through the years, he had determined that he would get a college
education. In 1937, at the age of twenty-six, he learned of a possible work
scholarship at Kentucky State College in Frankfort. He applied, and because of
his background and the hard work he had done, he was accepted. The scholarship
provided room, board, and tuition and $7.50 a month. In exchange, he worked
nearly full time on the college farm where he shared a house with eleven others.

His education again had to march in step with his required working hours,
and at long last he was awarded his long-sought college degree. He was able to
secure a teaching assignment in Scott County. By this time he had married, and to
meet his added responsibilities, he took a state job as a night-time janitor.

"Brown vs. School Board," the landmark civil rights case outlawing
segregated schools, delighted his heart and deflated his wallet. His job was

eliminated, and he had left only his janitorial work. He speaks of that time as going on and knowing that something better would turn up. It did.

At the time, many black orphans were living in state institutions. These children might have been placed in adoptive homes had the state been able to find such homes. An official called George to his office one day and asked if he felt he could find homes for these children within the Black Community. With his experience and knowledge, George was a natural. He accepted on the spot and became a social worker.

He traveled to every nook and cranny of the Commonwealth, speaking and encouraging people to open up their hearts an homes to these children so much in need of the love and affection of a family. Literally hundreds of children were placed into homes where they found love and encouragement because of this social worker. Many years later, he still hears from some of those whose lives he touched.

This writer knew Mr. Simmons years later when he was Assistant Supervisor of adoptions in the Child Welfare Department and is acquainted with the work that he did with children and the kindness and concern he showed for them.

He has been a leader in the Black Community and has long been active in the advancement of racial equality. Incidentally, he also served as president of our organization.

Life has never been easy for George Simmons, but it has forever been satisfying. Through it all he has persevered, and he has achieved a life of service to others. All the more remarkable when you think about the prospects of the little black boy born into the poverty of the Mississippi Delta over eight decades ago.

Thank you for your consideration,

James L. Peel

CONCERNED CITIZEN OF THE MONTH

1971

This month's concerned citizen is Mr. George W. Simmons, Jr. of Frankfort, Kentucky. Mr. Simmons is a youthful looking sixty-year-old husband, father of one and grandfather of two. Mr. Simmons graduated with a Bachelor of Science Degree from Kentucky State College in 1950. Since that time, he has carried his education to advanced studies at the University of Kentucky and the University of Louisville-Kent School of Social Work.

Mr. Simmons has taught Vocational Agriculture at the Lincoln Institute, Lincoln Ridge, Kentucky and at Ed Davis High School in Georgetown, Kentucky. He has also conducted adult Vocational Agriculture classes and supervised farm projects for both adults and high school boys who had projects in Vocational Agriculture. Mr. Simmons has also taught Science and Biology.

His social work career began as a child welfare worker, after which he became assistant supervisor of adoptions. Presently, Mr. Simmons, is Chief Employment Counselor in the Department of Economic Security. Under the supervision of Counseling and Program of Special Services, he serves as the State Handicapped Specialist, responsible for providing leadership and direction to the statewide program of services to the handicapped.

Mr. Simmons is an active member of many civic groups and clubs, and among these groups, he has been Co-Chairman of the Crusade for Children Drive for the past three years.

Mr. Simmons has, for the past nine years assisted inmates, from the Kentucky State Reformatory, who were eligible for parole or release, in finding places to live and employment. He has tried to keep in contact with the men he has helped, just in case they may need further assistance.

All of this work and help is done in his spare time and at his own expense, and the New Way staff would like to sincerely thank this month's concerned citizen, Mr. George W. Simmons, for his unselfish interest in his fellow man.

A FEW GOOD VOLUNTEERS

Able To Weather
Difficult Times

Friendly Smile

Helping Hands

Ready To Meet
Any Challenge

Willing To Take
That Extra Step

Dedicated To
Making A Difference

Healthcare is more than just about health. . . it's about caring.

For over 20 years, Bluegrass Regional Medical Center and the American Red Cross have been working hand in hand to provide caring, compassion, and comfort to patient's and their families. A great team of Red Cross Volunteers are on duty at Bluegrass Regional Medical Center year 'round. At BRMC, we know it takes a special person to donate their time and efforts to helping others and we appreciate this selfless contribution.

Our volunteers come in all ages, shapes, sizes and colors, but all have one thing in common. . . their commitment to others. *Could this be you?* Call now and find out more.

Don't miss this challenging opportunity to help others, contact the American Red Cross Office at 223-1795. Your thoughtfulness, concern and energy can make the difference. We need you.

Bluegrass REGIONAL MEDICAL CENTER

(formerly King's Daughter's Memorial Hospital)

American Red Cross

201 King's Daughters Drive • Frankfort, Kentucky 40601 • 502-875-5240   318 Washington Street • Frankfort, Kentucky 40601 • 502-223-1795

George Simmons Mark Marraccini

Simmons returns home to find he's come a long way from Jonestown

By MELISSA BELL
State Journal Staff Writer

A trip to his hometown for the first time in 54 years allowed George W. Simmons to see how far he had come.

The eldest son of a Baptist preacher, Simmons lived in Jonestown, Miss., until he was 22 years old. He still had two years of high school to complete. "In that vicinity that was common," he said.

He would start the school year and soon after be forced to drop out to help support the family. He eventually graduated high school when he was 25 years old in a small town in southeast Missouri.

He attended Kentucky State University where he worked his way through school on a 268-acre farm, tending the and, milking cows and delivering eggs for $7.80 a month. Despite teasing from classmates that he was too old to be in college, he received an agricultural degree from KSU and later a social work degree from the University of Louisville.

Throughout his life he worked as a teacher, social worker and state supervisor for adoption of the handicapped. Now 75 years old, Simmons is retired and lives with his wife Charlotte, a microbiologist with the state health department, on College Park Drive. Their home is located on a portion of the land he tilled in college.

Compared to most of his former Jonestown school friends, Simmons is a success. Many never completed high school and are still in Jonestown hanging around the streets Simmons said.

Not only have most of his hometown friends chosen "the low way" the town itself has gone by the wayside. When Simmons, along with about 200 other former Jonestown residents, returned for the town's first homecoming day on Sept. 7, he was disappointed to find that most of the buildings had dilapidated and little progress had taken place.

The town's population (about 1,00) is similar to when Simmons left except now it is composed primarily of blacks instead of both black and whites, he said.

One beer joint building "looked like it would fall in on you," Simmons said. The door appeared to be an old barn door and floorboards were loose, he said.

"I'm really very much concerned about it," Simmons said "When I went down there and saw it I began to wonder about the future of Jonestown.

"I was disappointed. They're far from what I expected. I expected them to have kept up their property a little better."

mons said. And for the first time in 100 years, a black, Mike Espy, was elected U.S. Congressman in 1986 to represent Mississippi's second congressional district.

Both officials spoke at a banquet in honor of the homecoming and Simmons presented each with Kentucky Colonel certificates. A telegram from Gov. Martha Layne Collins congratulating the town on its first homecoming and having elected its mayor to a third term was read aloud during the banquet and Simmons said he never felt so proud.

Simmons and his wife found time outside of homecoming activities, which included a parade, games, singing and dancing, to visit his childhood locales. The family's former home has since been demolished and replaced with a cotton patch. And now the cotton fields where he used to work are picked by one worker who operates a machine.

The visit reminded him of how hard he had worked to get to college so he could be better off than his parents. He was determined to get a college education because he wanted to be like his high school principal, J.H. McMillian. "My mother used to say I liked him so well I tried to walk like him," he said.

But his attempts to save money were often thwarted because his family needed his financial support. Once he tried to earn extra money by growing his own cotton on his cousin's land. His cousin wasn't charging him for the land and his parents were going to help him pick the cotton for free and the profit would be all his. But when it was harvest time, his parents desperately needed the money and he had to pay them to pick. He only cleared $3.15 and with that he bought a pair of shoes.

He was so disappointed after that incident that he set out to steal a white man's plow. He was going to sell it and keep the money for his schooling. But in the process of transporting it, the plow got stuck on a bridge and he had to leave it there for fear he would be caught and imprisoned.

He finally got a break when someone told him about Kentucky State University, a college that allowed students to work in exchange for tuition, room and board and meals. So he hitchhiked to Frankfort.

"I was so thankful I could see a little further and foresee the value of an education," Simmons said.

The George Simmons Family

The George Simmons house on College Park Drive built in 1964

DEPARTMENT OF ECONOMIC SECURITY

DIVISION OF CHILDREN'S SERVICES
FRANKFORT

August 27, 1956

Mr. George Simmons
316 East Main Street
Frankfort, Kentucky

Dear Mr. Simmons:

This is to advise that Mr. V. E. Barnes, Commissioner of the Department of Economic
Security, has authorized your appointment to the position of Social Worker, Grade 7,
with the Children's Services Division with headquarters in Frankfort, Kentucky, on a
probationary basis, at a salary of $280.00 a month, effective September 1, 1956.
Your assignment will be in District 11 as well as at Kentucky Village.

Please report to Mr. Luther Minyard in the Central Office on Tuesday, September 4, 195

According to the regulations of the Kentucky Merit System, under which agency this
Division operates, it is necessary that your appointment be for a probationary period
of six months prior to receiving permanent status in this position.

You will be allowed certain expenses in connection with your employment, concerning
which your supervisor, Mrs. Sarah S. Hammonds, will inform you. We should like to
further advise that your working hours will be from 8:00 a.m. to 4:30 p.m., Monday
through Friday.

Please stop by the Personnel Office of the Department of Economic Security on Tuesday
and complete the necessary forms in order that your name may be placed on the payroll.

We are looking forward to your association with us.

Sincerely yours,

Donald E. Lathrope
Director

cc: Mr. V. E. Barnes, Commissioner
    Mrs. Sarah S. Hammonds
    Miss Rosalyn King

BOOKER T. WASHINGTON
GRADE AND HIGH SCHOOL

C. B. NUCKOLLS, Principal

ASHLAND, KENTUCKY

November 12, 1957

Mr. Ernest P. Rall
State Supervisor of Adoption
Division of Children's Services
Capitol Annex
Frankfort, Kentucky

Dear Mr. Rall:

I am enclosing an article "Welfare Officer Confers" that appeared in the Sunday edition of our Ashland Daily Independent, Sunday, November 10th. Please check the article carefully and let us have your opinions and suggestions relative to our proposed plan of procedure in informing my people in the State Adoption Program for Negro Children.

I am very happy to advise you and the entire staff of our State Department that our own Mr. George Simmons, Assistant State Supervisor for the Adoption of Negro Children gave a very fine discussion of the method of the adoption of Negro children and especially emphasizing the urgent needs for the adoption of the large number of Negro children who are deserving of good homes.

I wish to congratulate you and the State Department in the appointment of Mr. Simmons, whom I have known across the years to be very efficient and capable and is making good in his work which reflects credit to his race and an asset to our State Department of Children's Welfare.

We cannot find words to express to our local workers, Mrs. America Holbrook and Miss Adams for the untiring cooperation and help they are according our group, briefly they are doing a fine job for everybody in this area.

Hoping to have a reply from you relative to our meeting and with best good wishes for your continued success, I am,

Very truly yours,

C. B. NUCKOLLS, Principal.

CBN/elw
Enclosure

BOOKER T. WASHINGTON
GRADE AND HIGH SCHOOL
C. B. NUCKOLLS, PRINCIPAL
ASHLAND, KENTUCKY

November 13, 1957

Mr. George W. Simmons
Assistant Supervisor
Department of Economic Security
Divison of Negro Child Adoption
Capitol Annex
Frankfort, Kentucky

Dear Mr. Simmons:

Please find enclosed news article as planned. I hope it
will meet with your approval.

Please check copies also enclosed.

You made a very fine impression and you are doing a good
job. Please write me upon receipt of this letter. With
best good wishes for your continued success.

Very truly yours,

C. B. NUCKOLLS, Principal.

CBN/elw

Enclosures.

November 19, 1957

Mr. C. B. Nuckolls, Principal
Booker T. Washington School
Ashland, Kentucky

Dear Mr. Nuckolls:

I appreciate very much your recent letter and the newspaper account of
Mr. Simmons' discussion with the Negro citizens of the Ashland area.

I think the plan of procedure in informing the people of your area of
the help that is available through our local child welfare office is
very good. I am sure this will be of valuable service to Mrs. Holbrook
and Miss Adams and they will appreciate your cooperation.

I further appreciate your words of encouragement of the work of this
Department, which is being done through Mrs. Holbrook, Mr. Simmons and
Miss Adams.

Thank you for the interest shown in our program and your cooperation with
Mrs. Holbrook, Mr. Simmons and Miss Adams.

Very truly yours,

Ernest F. Hall
Supervisor of Adoptions

bc: Mrs. Holbrook
    Miss Adams
    Mr. Simmons

A Determined Man

Old Mansion Looked Like Heaven To Him

By NETTIE GLENN

After sitting quietly on the hill for almost one-hundred years, the Kentucky State College is finally undergoing a vast and much needed building program. Established by the 1887 Legislature, it was called the State Normal School for Colored Persons and its object was teacher training.

To be admitted, a pupil had to be at least sixteen years old, healthy, of high moral character and sign a pledge to teach in the colored common schools for twice the time he attended the school.

The first president, J. H. Jackson, was a Berea College graduate who had taught school for many years in Kansas City, Missouri. In 1890 the departments

of agriculture, mechanics and domestic economy were added and the school's scope was broadened to include trades. At that time the college, with the exception of the mechanics building, was encompassed by one large turreted brick building. The women lived in a large dormitory and the men were housed in the remains of a once grand mansion located on the farm across the road.

By 1898 the annual state appropriation was a whopping $3,000.00 — that, plus 14½ per cent of the federal appropriations due Kentucky for agricultural and mechanical colleges was the school's entire operating capital.

Being an agricultural training institution was a distinct advantage because the farm was

utilized not only for teaching but to feed the student body and faculty.

Located high on a hill in a particularly beautiful part of this lush land stand the remains of the one-time elegant mansion which later became the men's domitory. When the land was purchased for the college the house was part of the deal. Facing sunshine, it overlooks a beautifully contoured valley and just below it, nestled close to the hill, is the old spring house that was the first waterworks for the college.

Viewed from the outside, the old mansion seems to be in pretty good condition but the interior has been neglected for so many years that it seems to be almost beyond recall.

The basement of this building is what poses the irony of the situation for located underneath this once-grand home are extensive slave quarters. Dark and dark, they send a shiver up the spine and make you want to dash back outside to the bright day.

Although this mansion may have represented slavery to many Negroes over a hundred years ago, it was emancipation to one lonely Negro man who arrived here from Caruthersville, Missouri, back in 1937.

George Simmons, Jr., was, and still is, a determined Negro who long ago realized that the real key to the freedom of his race, and other races, lies in education. He has spent a lifetime proving this philosophy.

George is the son of a Baptist preacher and the oldest of seven children. Missouri didn't offer many educational advantages to black people back when he was in school there and what was offered was hard to come by for George was constantly forced to leave school and help provide for his family. As a result, he wasn't graduated from high school until he was twenty-five years old.

George hitch hiked to Frankfort and entered Kentucky State College on April 2, 1937.

"This building looked like heaven to me then," he remarked, as he was showing us

George Simmons Points To A Window
Of The Old Slave Quarters In The Old Mansion

eemed to stand still. They were ich better off financially and in't have so many worries at me. Some days I worked so rd on the farm that I would fall eep studying."

In 1941 George married Mary zabeth Harris and they had son. In 1948 he started rking for the Department of Economic Security as janitor, a job he held for over eight years. His first real job was at Lincoln Ridge for $290.00 a month. After that his career spiraled and he is now a principal employment counselor for the Department of Economic Security. He and his wife are now living in a beautiful home in College Park sub-division.

The general feeling of the black community that resides in beautiful homes in the area is disappointment at seeing the old mansion razed. They believe it should be restored and main-tained in the grand manner of over a hundred years ago.

The slave quarters would also be restored — a grim reminder of a time mankind should never be allowed to forget.

But progress is seldom patient with the past and sometimes thus another world will soon become sacrificed to the almighty 'dozer, and reduced to dust.

Just as slavery has been.

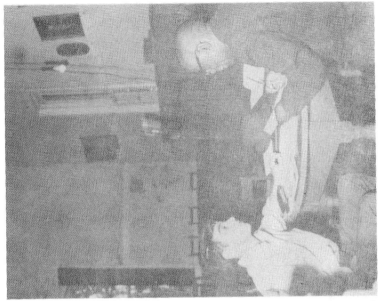

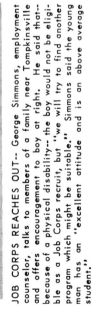

JOB CORPS REACHES OUT-- George Simmons, employment counselor, talks to members of a family near Tompkinsville and offers encouragement to boy at right. He said that-- because of a physical disability-- the boy would not be eligible as a Job Corps recruit, but "we will try to find another program which might be suitable." Simmons said the young man has an "excellent attitude and is an above average student."

TEMPORARY OFFICE-- A Job Corps applicant discusses possibilities of the program with Simmons at the Tompkinsville courthouse. This boy was partially physically disabled and not eligible. He said he really wanted a job.

SERVICES TO NEGRO CHILDREN IN KENTUCKY

By: George W. Simmons, Assistant Supervisor of Adoptions

For approximately two years it has been my privilege and pleasure to serve the Division of Children's Services and observe its keen interest in and growth of services to the Negro children of Kentucky. It has been a stimulating experience to serve the needs of humanity that have their reflections in the care and happiness of children. To bring happiness and security to children is truly christianity in action.

Philosophy and Policies:

To give every child an opportunity to develop to the fullest extent of his capabilities has always been an underlying philosophy of the Division's program. It is our policy to hold in strict confidence every adoption. Our processing techniques help establish desirable human relationships for all concerned, and are founded upon the guiding principals of faith, integrity, and sincerity.

George W. Simmons

During the past 2-1/2 years 30 Negro children were placed in adoptive homes by the Division. The Division approved 32 homes during the same period. Statistics concerning Negro adoption activity indicate that from 1951 thru 1955 thirty Negro children were placed and 36 homes approved. While it is evident there has been a decided numerical increase in Negro adoptive activities, there still remains much to be done.

To date, public information meetings have been held in seventy-one counties which contain the largest Negro population. This represents almost 9,000 miles traveled. There was a most cordial climate of acceptance on the part of each and every community visited. All contacts revealed a sharp interest in seeking information on adoptive practices, policies, procedures and clarification of false impressions relating to adoption. Many sincere childless couples left these meetings, seemingly with the ultimate desire for a child by adoption.

Many Child Welfare Workers and District Supervisors attended these meetings. They met the couples interested in obtaining a family through adoption. The workers presented a wonderful spirit of co-operation and showed their usual willingness to make their services available.

In many of the counties visited the County Social Services Committee had one or two Negro members. This is an indication that this Department as well as the Division of Children's Services is giving full recognition to all Kentucky citizens who may need public welfare services. The various committee members are Key people in their communities who are in a position to recognize the needs for services. They contributed their knowledge of community problems and potentials in many of the public information meetings concerning adoption and other services of the Division.

The Outlook:

There is much optimism as we advance forward in our program of adoption. The fine team concept that is generated in the various communities, the adult pride and desire for an approved home life for every child and the very fine spirit of the personnel of the Division all contribute toward a brighter future.

The second visit to some communities brought about more positive responses than the first. If the need exists, we will make additional contacts to gain more expert insight into Negro problems as to insure an applicable service to each race. Whether this will be a continued expansion of our Negro adoptive placement program, or all existing services offered by the Division we sincerely believe the needs will be met.

"Let's Give a Child a Chance to Live," "More Homes For More Needy Children," will continue to be the motto of the Division for Negro as well as other children.

* * *

Local Offices

CENTRAL OFFICE NEWS

FRANKFORT - Just as STABILITY was about to go to press our faithful and hard-working Patsy Trayner became ill. Her physician said she needed at least a months's rest before returning to work. Patsy has been burning the lamps long after most of us have gone home for the day — also on week ends. We sincerely hope Patsy will be feeling stronger soon — not just to help us with the work load — but because we like her.

BOWLING GREEN NEWS

BOWLING GREEN - The Bowling Green Office was honored to have four of the Cause II Project trainees in the office last fall for a four-week period. They were: Charles Oliver, Bowling Green; Dennis Jenkins, Bowling Green; Don Mayfield, Bowling Green; and John Thompson, New Haven.

The Bowling Green ES personnel enjoyed a party in their honor on October 8. Refreshments consisted of hot Russian tea and a large decorated jam cake.

We are happy to announce that Charles Oliver and Dennis Jenkins will remain in the Bowling Green Office as permanent employees. We also welcome Mrs. Shirley Towe and welcome back Miss Beverly Benson, who was a summer employee in our office. they will be working as part-time permanent employees in the UI section.   —By Barbara Kiel

COLUMBIA NEWS

COLUMBIA - Charles Rush, social service supervisor, was elected president of District 8, Kentucky Welfare Association.

We are glad to welcome Mrs. Gwendolyn Young to the Columbia Public Assistance office, as she recently received a promotion and a transfer from the Edmonton Public Assistance office.

RETURNS -- Back with DES after serving with Child Welfare is George W. Simmons, above. Simmons is now an employment counselor with the mobile team under the ES counseling section.

Mrs. Genevieve Glass was recently honored as being appointed a member of the South Central Area Development Council in Edmonton.

Mrs. Elizabeth Harper, at the advice of her physician, enjoyed a much needed leisurely rest in California during the fall of 1965.

The Barbourville Training Center recently has occupied one of our newer employees. Mrs. Sara Celsor accepted a position in the Monroe County Office as Service Worker. Another assignment in Monroe County has been accepted by Miss Saralu White, who took the position of clerk typist.

We are glad to hear that Mrs. Elsie Vaughn is back at home and recovering rapidly from a recent operation. Mrs. Vaughn is the mother of Judy Morrision, Adair County clerk typist.

—By Margie E. Collins

COVINGTON NEWS

COVINGTON - Thirty persons, including five visitors, attended a luncheon meeting of the Covington subchapter of IAPES on Thursday, January 27. We were to have Larry Mitchell and Grace Cook join us.

Mrs. Dorothy Cordray, president, introduced Mrs. Jeanne Bonham, northern Kentucky field director for the Greater Cincinnati Community Action Commission, the speaker, who explained that the commission is designed to fight poverty in Kenton, Boone and Camp-

bell counties as well as in Hamilton and Clermont counties in Ohio.

She emphasized that they are directing their efforts toward helping families become independent.

Her functions are to learn what can be done in Northern Kentucky to strengthen existing anti-poverty programs and to begin new projects. Mrs. Bonham said the Department of Economic Security — both Employment Service and Public Assistance — as well as other local agencies, would be asked to co-operate.

—By Marguerite NeCamp

DANVILLE NEWS

DANVILLE - Mrs. Frances M. Montgomery, supervisor, was called to Greensboro, N.C. not long ago because of the serious illness of her mother.

Edward Cecil, service worker in Marion County, recently completed training in Lexington.

Mrs. Louise Eddleman, field worker in Washington County, spent two weeks visiting her son in Florida.

Mrs. Dortha C. Smith, District Steno, took a trip to Memphis, Tenn. where she and her husband participated in a national singing convention.

Mrs. Octavia Shackleford, field worker in Boyle County, spent a few days in November visiting her grandson in Virginia. They visited many interesting places including Williamsburg and Jamestown.

The Danville District was indeed sorry to lose Mrs Betsy Votaw, stenographer in Washington County. Mrs. Votaw transferred to the Lexington District and is working in Versailles.

By Dortha C. Smith

Growing services of the Kentucky Department of Child Welfare call for growing numbers of social workers. Liberal arts majors are being recruited for in-service training programs.

July 19, 1978

Christopher W. Brady/Program Director
Audio Visual Centre
P.O. Box 188
LaGrange, Ky. 40031

George W. Simmons Jr. Chief
Chief Employment Counselor
Dept. of Economic Security
New Capital Annex
410 College Park Drove
Frankfort, Ky. 40221

Dear George,
       The Audio Visual Centre, which is located inside the Kentucky State
Reformatory, cordially invites you to visit our group on the evening of
September 7, 1978 in the capacity of guest speaker. We have some men in our
group that will be re-entering society soon and would appreciate any information that you could give. If you wish to bring someone along we request
that prior notice be given so as to process the appropriate clearance forms.

       Your time of arrival should be around 6:30 p.m. There will be an
escort waiting within the Administration Building. The program will be infor
mal, and will start at 7:00 p.m., and must conclude at 9:00 p.m. While pro-
gressing through your presentation please allow time for an question and
answer period. I am confident that you will find the time well spent and
enlightening as well as providing a program for our group.

       The Audio Visual Centre, composed of some forty members (inmates)
was organized to promote and broaden the cultural and social aspects of its
members. Through the use of educational films, lectures, and social activities,
including, periodic guest speakers we have added to the enthusiasm and
challenge of indiviual thinking.

       As all arrangements are subject to the approval of the Administration
we would appreciate a letter of acceptance or declination as soon as possible.
If you have any questions concerning this letter feel free to contact Mr.
David Vislisel, AV Centre Advisor.

                                        Sincerely Yours,

                                        Christopher W. Brady
                                        Program Director

cc: David Vislisel/AV Centre Advisor
Tele: 502-222-9441

COMMONWEALTH OF KENTUCKY
DEPARTMENT OF ECONOMIC SECURITY

LOUIE B. NUNN
GOVERNOR

FRANKFORT

MERRITT S. DEITZ, JR.
COMMISSIONER

November 3, 1971

Mr. George W. Simmons, Jr.
401 College Park Drive
Frankfort, Kentucky 40601

Dear Mr. Simmons:

May I, on the occasion of your being named to the
Employees' Honor Roll of Long-Time Service, extend to you
congratulations.

The very fact that you have been a state employee
for 23 years plus attests to your capability and
dependability. During those years, your influence must
have made itself felt in many positive and constructive
ways.

You may look forward, I am certain, to even better
days ahead. In doing so, you have not only my best wishes
but also those of many fellow-employee friends.

Sincerely,

Charles M. Karcher
Deputy Commissioner

Henry Clay High School

2100 FONTAINE ROAD

Lexington, Kentucky 40502

TELEPHONE (606) 269-3326

October 8,1975

Mr. George W.Simmons, Jr.
401 College Park Drive
Frankfort,Kentucky 40601

Dear Mr. Simmons:

Thank you very much for your help and interest
in my son Herschel. Thank you also for the delay
in receiving your compensation for service rendered.

Regards to your wife.

Thanks again and may God continue to bless you.

Sincerely,

Norman L.Passmore

CABINET FOR HUMAN RESOURCES
COMMONWEALTH OF KENTUCKY
FRANKFORT 40621

DEPARTMENT FOR HEALTH SERVICES   April 2, 1984

Ms. Shelly Patrick
Capital Plaza Hotel
Frankfort, Ky. 40601

Dear Ms. Patrick:

    I wanted to let you know what an enjoyable experience it was holding
our conference at the Capital Plaza Hotel on March 27-29, 1984. The entire
hotel seemed to go out of its way to accommodate our requirements.

    Specifically, I would like to commend Mr. Randy Louvelle and Mr. George
Simmons. Both Randy and George were always close by yet never obvious
in their attention. It made our staff much more comfortable knowing that
first, they would be there when needed, and even more important that they
could handle any request we made. So often you can find someone but that
someone is powerless to help.

    Again, my compliments to the hotel and its staff. We look forward
to future meetings to be held at the Capital Plaza Hotel.

                                    Sincerely,

                                    Charles W. Gollmar

                                    Charles W. Gollmar
                                    Program Coordinator
                                    Kentucky Diabetes Control Program

CWG:mg

130 West State Street
Frankfort, Kentucky   40601

May 17, 1984

Mr. Michael Richmond, Manager
Capital Plaza Hotel
405 Wilkinson Boulevard
Frankfort, Kentucky   40601

Dear Mr. Richmond:

  I would like to take this opportunity to thank
you and your colleagues for the beautiful hotel you
have brought into existence, and for the selection of
George W. Simmons, Jr., to be (I think) in charge of
employees on the main floor. He has always been so
gracious, intelligent, pleasant, and thoughtful of the
needs of others. I feel so grateful when I see him
directing visitors to the hotel.

  You have been very successful, it seems to me,
in the selection of your personnel.

  Thank you again, sir.

Most sincerely,

Margaret Willis

MARGARET WILLIS

MAIN HEADQUARTERS
Fifth Floor, 55 W. Jackson Blvd.
Chicago 60604
322-1983

GEORGE W SIMMONS
401 COLLEGE PARK DR
FRANKFORT   KY 40601

June 3, 1983

Dear GEORGE W SIMMONS

Thank you for your kind assistance and contribution to my recent Mayoral campaign.

Your commitment and loyalty were deeply appreciated.

I trust that I can continue to count on your support in the months and years ahead.

Sincerely,

Harold Washington
Mayor

HW/hm

Kentucky Department of Education

Alice McDonald, Superintendent of Public Instruction
Capital Plaza Tower, Frankfort, Kentucky 40601

February 2, 1984

Mr. Michael Richmond, Manager
Capital Plaza Hotel
405 Wilkinson Boulevard
Frankfort, Kentucky 40601

Dear Mr. Richmond:

I would like to commend one of your employees for being one of the best public relations experts I have met. Mr. George Simmons is a walking advertisement for the Capital Plaza Hotel. On two separate occasions he has made my guests and me feel very welcome in the new hotel by giving us a grand tour of your facilities.

Mr. Simmons' engaging personality and hospitality made our visit very special, and I wanted you to know what a valuable employee you have in Mr. Simmons.

I have been impressed with all of the features of the hotel and am looking forward to working with you and Mr. Bob Stephens on the little meeting I have scheduled for April.

Best wishes for continued success.

Sincerely,

Lydia Wells Sledge, Director
Unit for Educational Improvement

LWS:dh

When our schools work, Kentucky works.

June 7, 1984

Dear Manager,

We spent last weekend at your hotel and had a delightful time. The hotel is just beautiful and we hope to return! The highlight of our trip was meeting your bell-captain, George Simmons. He was a genuine, articulate, thoroughly delightful gentleman. We've been to scores of hotels and have never met anyone as caring or charming as George was. He left us with a delightful poem: "It's your attitude not your aptitude that determines your latitude." What a powerful thought! Too bad we don't have a few more George Simmons to go around. You are fortunate to have him in your hotel.

Best of luck to you in the future.

Sincerely

Wilkinson'87

December 17, 1986

Mr. George W. Simmons, Jr.
401 College Park Drive
Frankfort, Kentucky 40601

Dear George,

May I take this opportunity to thank you for your friendship and generosity.

The confidence and support you have shown in my candidacy means a great deal to me and will long be remembered. With friends such as you behind this effort, I know we will be successful.

With best personal regards,

Sincerely yours,

Wallace G. Wilkinson

WGW:amh

P.S. I am enclosing a Wilkinson '87 pin. I hope you'll wear it often and proudly.

MAILED SEPARATELY

1230 HIGHWAY 127 SOUTH ▪ FRANKFORT, KENTUCKY 40601 ▪ 502-875-1987

Paid for by Wilkinson for Governor Committee, Asa Hord, Treasu